the A to Z of DREAMS

the A to Z of DREAMS

Michael Johnstone

Capella

Published by
Arcturus Publishing Limited
for Bookmart Limited
Registered Number 2372865
Trading as Bookmart Limited
Desford Road
Enderby
Leicester
LE19 4AD

This edition published 2002

© Arcturus Publishing Limited
Unit 26/27 Bickels Yard
151-153 Bermondsey Street
London SE1 3HA

ISBN 1-84193-132-2

Author: Michael Johnstone
Editor: Rebecca Panayiotou
Text designer: Zeta Fitzpatrick @ Moo Design
Cover designer: Alex Ingr

Printed and bound in Finland

Contents

Introduction

Skilfully used, the very word, 'dream' has the power to move us hugely. This was nowhere more evident than at a civil rights rally in Washington in 1962 when American evangelist Martin Luther King brought tears to countless thousands of eyes and cheers to countless thousands of throats by prefacing his visions of society with the words, 'I have a dream'.

We all have dreams. They are things we all experience but few of us understand.

Dreams are things most of us dismiss as the meaningless meandering of our sleeping minds.

Dreams are things that take us into a world where the grotesque and the fantastic merge with the formal and everyday to create a kaleidoscope of images and experiences; a realm in which pleasure can turn into terror and logic surrender to chaos in one rapid eye movement.

But dreams are something that can be interpreted and understood. They may meander but they are far from

●●●●●●●●●●●●●●●●●●●●●●●●●●●●●●●●●●●

meaningless. As Jonathan Swift, the chronicler of Lemuel Gulliver's travels to fantastic lands put it, 'To dream is nothing else but to think sleeping.' But while we can often (but not always) control our waking thoughts, we are unable to control our sleeping ones. That does not mean that we should dismiss them: indeed, some of the greatest minds of the nineteenth and twentieth centuries explored the world of dreams and used them to explain the psychological conditions of those who sought their help.

Dreams as Old as Time

Societies older than ours used the dreams of dreamers to predict the future. Five thousand years ago, the dreamers of Babylon were describing their dreams and ways of interpreting and recording them on clay tablets. A thousand years later the Ancient Egyptians painted pictograms on their papyruses and on their pyramid walls to detail what they had dreamed about during their sleeping hours.

A thousand years after that the Hindus wrote accounts of their dreams in the *Vedas*. They believed that their dreams plugged them into a world of universal symbols associated with Hindu gods and demons.

Like the *Vedas,* the Bible, too, is full of dreamers,

● ●

including Jacob who, according to the Book of Genesis, was on his way to Padanaram when he grew tired and lay down to sleep, laying his head on a pillow of stones. As he slept he dreamed of a ladder reaching all the way from Earth to Heaven and being used by angels to move from one realm to the other. When he awoke he declared that, 'This is the house of God and this is the gate of Heaven.'

Jacob's son, Joseph was another famous dreamer who, in the words of modern lyricist Tim Rice, told the Pharaoh that:

> 'All those dreams you saw in your pyjamas
> Were the long-range forecast for the farmers.'

Joseph, Jacob's eleventh and favourite son, had the ability not only to recall his vivid dreams and understand what they meant, he could also interpret the dreams of others. Unfortunately for him two of his dreams almost cost him his life. In the first one, the corn sheaves his brothers were shaping bowed down and worshipped him, making him believe that he was better than his brothers. In the second, he dreamed that the sun, moon and eleven stars were bowing to him, making him even more arrogant than he had already become. His brothers came to dislike him intensely – intensely enough to plot to kill him. But later,

A-Z OF DREAMS

• •

they spared his life and sold him into slavery instead. After rebutting the advances of his master's wife, Joseph was cast into prison where one of the prisoners was the Pharaoh's butler whose dreams he correctly interpreted. When the butler was released, as Joseph had prophesied, he told the Pharaoh about the remarkable talents of his cellmate and when the king started to experience a recurring dream, he called for Joseph to be brought to him. The young man interpreted the royal dreams and when what he said came true, he became the Pharaoh's favourite and rose in rank and wealth.

The Book of Judges tells the story of how Gideon was guided by a dream. As the Israelites were making ready to launch an attack on their enemies, the Midianites, one of the soldiers who had been sleeping woke up. He stirred his comrades and said, 'Behold, I dreamed a dream and lo, a cake of barley bread tumbled into the host of Mideon and came unto a tent and smote it that it fell, and overturned it that the tent lay along.' The loaf of barley was interpreted as representing Gideon who was a miller by trade and it was he who led the Israelites to victory.

The Book of Daniel relates the story of Nebuchadnezzar who on waking from dream-filled

• •

sleep, summoned his astrologers, sorcerers and wise
men and demanded that they interpret his dreams.
'I have dreamed a dream and my spirit was troubled
to know the dream,' he said. When asked to describe
what he had dreamed, the king was unable to recall
the details but demanded that they proceed to
interpret them anyway – on pain of death! It was
Daniel who saved the day. He asked for time and went
home to sleep. Then, according to the scripture, 'was
the secret revealed unto Daniel in a night vision.' The
prophet duly returned to Nebuchadnezzar and
interpreted the forgotten dream, so saving his own
life and that of his colleagues!

The New Testament, too, has its share of prophetic
dreamers. According to St Matthew's gospel, 'The
angel of the Lord appeared unto him [Joseph] in
dream saying, Joseph, thou son of David, fear not to
take unto thee Mary for thy wife; for that which is
conceived in her is of the Holy Ghost.' Joseph was
warned in subsequent dreams that because Herod
was planning to kill Jesus, Joseph should take Mary
and the child into Egypt. And when it was safe to
return to Israel, the angel again appeared in a dream
saying, 'Arise, and take the young child and his mother
and go into the land of Israel, for they are dead which
sought the young child's life.'

A-Z OF DREAMS

But perhaps the most famous New Testament dream is Pilate's wife's. When the Roman governor was sitting in judgement over Jesus, he received word from his wife, saying, 'Have nothing to do with that just man, for I have suffered many things this day in a dream because of him.' Ignoring this prophetic warning, Pilate released Barabas and confirmed that the Crucifixion should proceed.

Dreams played a vital part in the founding of Islam for the prophet Mohamed received his divine calling in a dream that came to him from the one god, Allah. This was the first of many dreams and visions that he had involving the archangel Gabriel reading divine messages from a book. Unable to read or write himself, the prophet asked his wife Khadijah to record them for him. What she wrote is now preserved in the Koran, a true copy of the Heavenly Book and therefore unquestionable. Today, many followers of Islam interpret their good dreams as a gift from Allah that presage a physical reward. Bad dreams, they believe, are devil-sent and that to divulge them would bring about bad luck.

More modern dreamers include fifteenth-century farm girl Jeanne d'Arc who dreamed when she was thirteen that Saints Michael, Catherine and Margaret were bidding her to rescue the Paris region from English domination and went on to blaze her way into the history books as Joan of Arc.

Dreams Can Come True

Before then and since then, there are hundreds if not thousands of people who claim that their lives have been changed by being prewarned in a dream of some impending disaster. In 1912, when news of the sinking of RMS *Titanic* broke, for example, there were countless reports of people who had cancelled their passage because they had dreamed that the ship sank.

Similarly, when *Hindenberg*, the famous German airship, exploded in New Jersey in 1937, killing all aboard, there were many who claimed to having been prewarned in a dream.

Sadly, for every person whose life has been saved by a dream, there are those whose dreams came true who were powerless to take any action.

In 1865, one such dreamer wrote, 'About ten days ago I retired very late, I had been up waiting for important dispatches from the front. I could not have been in bed long when I fell into a slumber, for I was weary. I soon began to dream. There seemed to be a death-like

• •

stillness about me. Then I heard subdued sobs, as if a number of people were weeping. I thought I left my bed and wandered downstairs. There the silence was broken by the same pitiful sobbing, but the mourners were invisible. I went from room to room; no living person was in sight, but the same mournful sounds of distress met me as I passed along. It was light in all the rooms: every object was familiar to me: but where were all the people who were grieving as if their hearts would break? I was puzzled and alarmed. What could be the meaning of all this? Determined to find the cause of a state of things so mysterious and so shocking, I kept on until I arrived at the East Room, which I entered. There I met with a sickening surprise. Before me was a catafalque, on which was rested a corpse wrapped in funeral vestments. Around it were stationed soldiers who were acting as guards: and there was a throng of people, some gazing mournfully upon the corpse whose face was covered, others weeping pitifully. "Who is dead?" ' I demanded of one of the soldiers. "The President!" was his answer: "He was killed by an assassin!" Then came a loud burst of grief from the crowd, which awoke me from my dream.'

A few days later the dreamer Abraham Lincoln, went to the theatre and was assassinated by John Wilkes Booth!

● ●

Science, too, has its share of dreamers, including the German chemist, Friedrich Kekule von Stradonitz whose dreams led him to discover the cyclical structure of benzine.

Same Dreams: Different Cultures

Although everyone in the world has dreams, they mean different things to different cultures. Canadian Inuits, for example, believe that when they are asleep, their souls leave their bodies to live in a dream world. They firmly believe that a sleeper must never be roused, for if they awaken unexpectedly from sleep, their souls will still be in Dream World and can never be recovered.

The Hudson Bay Inuits are not alone in believing that the soul separates from the body during sleep. Natives of Greenland and some tribes in Papua New Guinea share this idea. They believe that their dreams are the souls' adventures during the bodies' sleeping hours.

In some parts of Africa a similar belief is so strongly held that a tribesman who wakes with a stiff leg may well be convinced that he has been injured in a dream battle.

Also in Africa, Zulus believe that some of them are born to receive prophetic messages from their ancestors,

• •

which come to them as dreams. The Zulu word for
these mystics translates as 'Dreamhouse'.

Some Kurds who cling to traditional beliefs, are
convinced that if they dream of something valuable,
they can claim it from whomever they encounter who
has it, using as much force as necessary. And if that
sounds like opportunism, it's nothing compared to the
belief held by the people of Kamchatka in Russia
whose men claim that if a man dreams of being
granted sexual favours by a girl he knows, it is her duty
to have sex with him. Curiously, women who dream of
having sex with men of their acquaintance are not
allowed to claim similar rights on their menfolk!

Dreams were vital to the Native American way of life.
Not only did their wise men interpret them and use
their meaning to predict the future or to make
decisions as to when to move from one hunting
ground to the next, dreams also played an important
part in the initiation of adolescent boys into adulthood.
Youngsters who claimed to have had especially vivid
dreams were, in some tribes, initiated at an earlier age
than their contemporaries whose dreams were
unremarkable or forgotten on awakening. And it was
no good for a youth to boast of dreams he had not
dreamt. All claimants were subject to strict inquisition

● ●

by elders and wise men, and it was only when these sages were convinced of the dreamer's veracity that he was allowed to be initiated along with others older, but not wiser, than he.

In pre-Communist China, there was a widespread belief that dreams could be used to foretell the future, but the same dreams could have different meaning for different dreamers. The interpretation put on it depended on the dreamers' state of health, the time of the dream, how long they had been asleep for and the astrological sign they were born under.

Dreams in Mythology and Literature

The worlds of mythology and literature are full of dreams and dreamers and have been for thousands of years. One of the earliest important pieces of written literature – perhaps the first – dates from the third millennium BC. Relating the life of the king of Mesopotamia, *The Epic of Gilgamesh* is punctuated with the dreams of its eponymous hero, and his friend Enkidu.

Enkidu first appears in a dream to Gilgamesh symbolized as a meteor falling from the sky, and later his arrival is heralded by a dream of an axe to which Gilgamesh is mysteriously drawn.

A-Z OF DREAMS

●●●●●●●●●●●●●●●●●●●●●●●●●●●●●●●●●●●●

During their subsequent adventures, the two experience many prophetic dreams most of which needed interpretation.

The dream messages related in Homer's *Iliad* and *Odyssey* required no interpretation: they were comparatively straightforward (as dreams go). Perhaps the most famous of these legendary Greek dreams is that of Penelope, Odysseus's wife and mother of Telemachus.

When the Greek hero is presumed lost, never to return, Penelope learns of a plot to kill Telemachus who has sailed off in search of his father. Distraught, Penelope begs the goddess Athene to save her son. One night, as Penelope sleeps, the goddess appears in her dream and assures her that Telemachus will be safe. 'How about Odysseus?' Penelope asks. 'Is he still alive, or is he now in the Halls of Hades?'

Athene refuses to be drawn, but drawing comfort from her dream, Penelope is convinced that her husband is still alive and will return to her. Many suitors seek her hand and anxious not to offend any of them in case she needs their assistance in the future, Penelope says she will remarry when she finishes the embroidery on which she is working. Such is her faith in her dream that every night in the secrecy of her chamber, she unpicks what she has done that day to ensure that the work will never be done. And she is rewarded when Odysseus eventually comes home.

Ancient Greek and Latin writers from Hesiod in 700BC to Virgil who died in 19BC often drew on the dream world for inspiration. Hesiod called them 'daughters of the night', while Virgil wrote that they were a gift from the spirits of the dead who sent them from the Underworld to sleepers. His writings tell us that dreams that came true were sent through a gate crafted from horn while false dreams floated out through a gate carved in ivory.

The Greek author Plutarch wrote that pleasant dreams are like rays of light rebounding from good philosophy, while bad dreams are broken waves beating upon the rocks and craggy banks of the sleeping mind.

It was to Plutarch that William Shakespeare often turned for inspiration so, perhaps not surprisingly, the Bard's work is peppered with dreams. In *Richard III*, the Duke of Clarence tells of a dream of drowning that stayed with him for many days: and as every schoolboy used to know, the unfortunate duke met his sad end in a butt of Malmsey wine.

A-Z OF DREAMS

In *A Midsummer Night's Dream*, the lovelorn Hermia dreams that a serpent is eating at her ear while her swain, Lysander, looks on, uncaring. When she awakes, she finds that the unfaithful young man has abandoned her for another.

And in *Julius Caesar,* the great Roman general tells a fellow senator that his (Caesar's) wife, Calpurnia, had dreamed that his statue was spouting blood and taking this as an ill omen had begged him not to venture out of doors. Unfortunately, the confidant is one of the men plotting to assassinate Caesar and tells him that Calpurnia had misinterpreted the dream and that it is, in fact, a good omen.

Centuries later, H. G. Wells wrote a sinister story about a perfectly healthy man who dreams that he reads his obituary in the morning paper and when he wakes up is able to recall the date, a few weeks hence, on which it was published. His doctor assures him that he is in perfect health and good for many more years. But as the day draws nearer and nearer, the unfortunate dreamer can think of nothing else and becomes so agitated that his heart gives out as the appointed day dawns.

●●●●●●●●●●●●●●●●●●●●●●●●●●●●●●●●●●●●●

But perhaps the most famous 'dream' story was written by Wells' contemporary, Lewis Carrol, whose *Alice's Adventures in Wonderland* and *Alice Through the Looking Glass* take the reader into the quixotic world of a little girl who falls asleep on one hot summer's day.

Several writers have not only written about dreams, they have dreamed the plots and characters of some of their books. Samuel Taylor Coleridge, for example, claimed that many of the lines for his epic poem *Kubla Khan*, came to him in a dream, while Mary Shelley dreamed of a monster one night when she was visiting Italy with her husband and some of his friends.

'I saw – with eyes shut, but with acute mental vision – I saw the pale student of unhallowed arts kneeling beside the thing he had put together.' Believing that 'What terrified me will terrify others,' and everyone in the party having agreed to write a ghost story, she later said, 'I need only describe the spectre which had haunted my pillow.' The next day she announced, 'I have thought of a story,' and set to work. When it was finished everyone was so impressed with it that they persuaded her that the manuscript should be sent to a publisher. The book was *Frankenstein*, possibly one of the greatest Gothic horror stories of all time and the inspiration for a string of famous films.

Another novelist who dreamed the plot of one of his most famous works later wrote, 'I can give an instance or so of what part is done sleeping and what part awake… I had long been trying to write a story on this subject. For two days I went about wracking my brains for a plot of any sort and on the second night I dreamed a scene at the window and a scene afterward split in two in which, pursued for some crime, a man took a powder and underwent a change in the presence of his pursuers.' The writer was Robert Louis Stevenson and the book his dream inspired was *The Strange Case of Dr Jekyll and Mr Hyde*.

Some Famous Dream Interpreters

Sigmund Freud

It is hardly surprising that many people have turned their attention to trying to interpret our dreams. Perhaps the most famous was Sigmund Freud, the Austrian psychologist.

Born in Moravia in 1856, Freud studied medicine in Vienna, specializing first in neurology, later in psychopsychology. He was at the forefront of using hypnosis to help him solve his patients' problems, but later abandoned this in favour of 'free association' which allowed those who sought his help to express their thoughts in a state of what he called 'relaxed consciousness'. After years spent interpreting the childhood and dream recollections of his patients, Freud became convinced that dreams are the disguised manifestations of repressed sexual wishes. In 1900 he published his findings in *The Interpretation of Dreams*.

Although many of his theories are now widely discounted by psychologists, the book was for a while one of the most influential psychological manuals,

A-Z OF DREAMS

despite the fact that it took eight years to sell 600 copies and Freud received the princely sum of around £150 for the first edition. By the time he died, in 1939, he had made a great deal more from his writings.

Freud, who claimed that dreams were 'the royal road to the unconscious', maintained that the human mind operated on three levels – the Id, the Ego and the Super-ego. The Id, the unconscious pleasure principle, drives us to act as we desire. The Super-ego restrains us reminding us (unconsciously) of the strictures of society, the restraining voice of society (perhaps less relevant in these more permissive times than in the prim and proper days of Imperial Vienna) and of our own morality. The Ego tries to balance between the two, mediating between pleasure-seeking Id and the disapproving voice of the Super-ego.

History does not tell us if Freud read Stevenson's *Dr Jekyll and Mr Hyde*. Perhaps if he had he would have recognized the murderous Mr Hyde character as standing for the author's Id, respectable Dr Jekyll as his Super-ego, and the observers to the horrifying events as his Ego.

Briefly, Freud's theory can be summed up as follows:

SOME FAMOUS DREAM INTERPRETERS

• •

(a) Dreams are the fulfilment of wishes.

(b) But because we are conditioned by hundreds of influences, our dreams come to us in disguised form. So, dreaming that we are in a ship, for example, does not mean that we want to sail. The ship is the brain's metaphor for something else.

(c) Usually, this disguised metaphor represents the fulfilment of a wish that we are ashamed of, frightens us or that we have suppressed for some other reason.

(d) And finally, the wish is not something that has only recently been desired and repressed. Dreams are the disguised fulfilment of a wish we have been suppressing since childhood.

Modern psychologists now dispute Freud's research and conclusions – dreams, they say are the random imaginings of the resting brain. But to those of us who believe that dreams are important and can be properly interpreted, Freud still presents a lucid argument for his theories. We continue to believe that, in his words, 'The dreamer does know what his dream means, only he does not know that he knows it and, for that reason, thinks he does not know it.'

A-Z OF DREAMS

●●●●●●●●●●●●●●●●●●●●●●●●●●●●●●●●●●●●●

Carl Gustav Jung

Jung (1875 – 1961) was a psychologist who started out as a follower of Freud, but who later came to formulate his own theory of dreaming. He proposed that beneath the Id, Ego and Super-ego lies another layer of consciousness, which he called, 'the collective consciousness'. While Freud believed that dream symbols were fixed, Jung proposed that they varied according to the dreamer. In talking to his patients about their dreams, and reading about the dreams of long-dead men and women, he noticed that dreams tended to have a narrative structure containing images, figures and experiences. He called these 'archetypes' and believed that while they vary from dreamer to dreamer, they alert us to some aspect of our lives of which, in our waking lives, we are not aware.

According to Jungian theory, archetypes are the ancient and unconscious source of much of what we do and say. They are the patterns that shape our preconceptions of the world. We inherit them at birth as blank pages that we fill in according to the experiences we encounter as we make our way through life.

Some experts compare archetypes to animals' instincts: just as a bird knows how to build a nest

● ●

without being taught how to, so we inherit our archetypes and store them in our subconscious minds.

Archetypes are neither good nor bad. They live at the roots of our psyche in their raw, primitive state making their presence felt in our dream world.

The Mother

In its positive form, the Mother Archetype can appear as a traditional mother figure – mother, caring aunt or loving grandmother – or as a cave or place of worship that may be symbolic of the womb. Jung associated this archetype with connotations of material comfort and sympathy, growth, nourishment and fertility.

In its negative form, the Mother Archetype may appear as a witch or a dragon, indeed anything with associations with darkness or secrecy, manipulation or destruction, the poisonous or seductive.

The Father

This reflects the dreamer's role in life, his destiny and desire for success. In its positive form it represents protection and lawgiving: its negative side can be destructive and violent.

A-Z OF DREAMS

● ●

The Child

When the Child Archetype appears in dreams it often signposts a desire for significant change in the dreamer's life. Things forgotten or dismissed from childhood may need to be re-integrated to effect the subconsciously desired change.

The Anima

In males, the Anima (the word means 'soul' in Latin) represents the female aspect of the psyche and will manifest itself in the shape of a mermaid or goddess when maternal, intuitive qualities need to be addressed in some way. Doing so enables a man to achieve a more balanced and spiritual life. Appearing negatively, it suggests that the dreamer is moody and irritable and needs to take steps to address these adverse character traits.

The Animus

Just as the Anima represents the female attributes in the male psyche, so the Animus is representative of the male aspect of the female personality. Positively it lends itself to such male qualities as strength, rational, unemotional thinking, while negatively it suggests that the dreamer is manipulative, argumentative and over-opinionated.

SOME FAMOUS DREAM INTERPRETERS

The Persona

This is the part of ourselves that we want the world to see and acknowledge. It is our ego and reflects our consistency with what we believe that to be.

The Shadow

The same sex as the dreamer, the shadow is the repressed, dark side of the psyche, something not generally acknowledged by the dreamer. But if it is so acknowledged, it can allow dreamers to see themselves as others see them, and if they do not like what the shadow tells them, they can try to make appropriate changes.

While it is for the archetypes that Jung is mainly remembered, he also worked on the theory of 'big' and 'little' dreams. In big dreams there is a sense of what one writer has described as 'a sense of temporal and spatial infinity and speed and an extension of movement'. Such dreams are significant and, drawing on the collective unconsciousness, can presage significant events. Jung himself experienced several big, precognitive dreams about World War II. Big dreams are also concerned with personal issues such as family and health, work and relationships. Small dreams, Jung believed, were of little importance. They were little more than the subconscious having a clean

● ●

out, ridding itself of insignificant details and memories that were clogging it up, in much the same way that useless pieces of fluff can clog up a washing machine, preventing it from doing its job properly.

Fritz Perls

A near contemporary of Jung's, Perls (1893 – 1970) believed that dreams are more to do with the events of our lives rather than the struggles of our unconscious. He thought that everything we dream – every image and event, every fear and anxiety – reveals the shape of the individual (what he called 'the gestalt') rather than any collective unconscious.

He believed that there were three spectrum awarenesses in all our lives. At one end of this spectrum was an awareness of the self and at the other was an awareness of the world. Sandwiched between the two was a zone of fantasy that prevented the self and the world being at one with each other. It was this that manifested itself in our dreams. He encouraged his patients to role play their dreams, believing that the characters in a dream represent parts of the dreamer that have to be confronted or questioned, the aim being to integrate all the separate parts of the personality.

SOME FAMOUS DREAM INTERPRETERS

● ●

Perls believed that every detail of every dream – the characters dreamed of, the mood the dream created and every object dreamed, no matter how small and of apparent insignificance – **did** have significance. By talking about them when awake and by what Perls called 'setting up encounters between them', the dreamer could reach a deeper understanding of himself beyond surface perceptions.

Calvin S. Hall

Research into dreams and dream interpretation continued with Calvin S. Hall, an American psychologist whose initial area of speciality was behavioural traits in rats and if and how these could be interpreted and used to explain some behavioural traits in humans. Gradually he became more and more fascinated with dreams and using anonymous accounts of dreaming. Rather than try to interpret dreams for their precise meaning, Hall and, later, a colleague Robert Van de Castle, developed a method of coding dreams that many psychologists use today. Using Hall's approach, dreams are analysed for themes and patterns. He divided dreams into those concerning characters, those mainly to do with emotions, those about interactions, dreams about misfortune, dreams where

A-Z OF DREAMS

● ●

objects were the dominating theme and those where the setting was all-important.

The argument regarding the psychological interpretation of dreams persists. There are those who take an existentialist view, arguing that individuals choose for themselves, either consciously or subconsciously, what they want to be. Dreams are therefore wish-fulfilment – we construct our own waking lives: we construct our own sleeping ones, too.

Although we now know more about sleep than our ancestors did thousands of years ago, by and large, our dreams remain a mystery to us. But there is no doubt that in attempting to find out what they mean we can learn more about ourselves and, perhaps, more about what lies in store.

So welcome to the world of dreams and dreamers.

To Sleep...

We all suffer from the occasional sleepless night, hour after hour when we toss and turn desperate to drop off, and no sooner have we done so than the alarm goes and it's time to get up – woozy and ill-tempered. For sleep is something we all need but very often don't get enough of. It's essential for the repair of the body and for regenerating cells. If we don't get enough sleep we can become ill both physically and mentally.

Recent research has suggested that most of us need seven hours sleep every night. Much less or much more and we suffer. There are exceptions: Margaret Thatcher, British prime minister from 1979 until 1990, is said to have thrived on just four hours sleep each night. Winston Churchill on the other hand, took to his bed at least twice a day for an hour or two, and also had the ability to cat-nap – drop off for a few minutes and wake up refreshed and ready for action.

But there's more to sleep than simply closing our eyes and floating off to the Land of Nod. It's a complicated process that can be broken into several distinct stages. During the first stage, sleepers start to relax

• •

and drift in and out of a light doze from which they are easily awakened.

Real sleep begins to come in the second stage, but even then the sleeper can still be aroused relatively easily. Not so during stage three sleep when he or she is in a state of deep relaxation and can only be awakened by being shaken roughly or by a loud noise.

During stage four sleep much of our daily output of growth hormone, which helps in the process of repairing body tissue, is released.

Stage four completed, the process is reversed but rather than waking up on returning to stage one, the sleeper enters a new phase known as REM (Rapid Eye Movement) sleep and it's during this stage that most dreams are dreamt. REM sleep over, the sleeper returns to stage one and the whole cycle is repeated, four or five times a night, each complete cycle taking a little longer than an hour and a half.

REM sleep was first noted in the early 1950s by a researcher who noticed that at certain times during sleep, the eyes of the sleeping volunteer could be seen stirring beneath the closed eyelids. It was, the researcher thought, as if the sleeper's eyes were following movements.

A few years later two scientists, Eugene Aserinsky and Nathaniel Kleitman, published their research into the subject. They had found that during REM sleep the blood flow to the brain, which was raised in temperature, was increased, the sleepers, both male and female, became sexually aroused physically, and electrodes measuring the brain's activity showed distinctive patterns.

When sleepers were wakened up during REM sleep, they almost invariably recalled that they had been dreaming vividly, whereas about half of those awakened during N (non) REM sleep said that their dreams were more like daydreams.

The length of REM sleep increases with every cycle, the major muscle groups seeming to become almost paralysed each time the sleeper enters this phase. Some researchers believe that this is the body's way of protecting itself from injury or uncontrolled movements during sleep.

Subsequent research suggests that we need NREM

● ●

sleep in order to rest and for various vital body functions such as growth to take place and that REM sleep is more psychologically important.

People who don't get enough NREM sleep look obviously tired and become clumsy, while those deprived of REM sleep seem unable to concentrate on even the most everyday task and become emotional and oversensitive and often suffer memory loss.

Perchance to Dream

Dreams have been defined as the manifestation of conscious thoughts, feelings and images during sleep when conscious activity is usually in a state of complete suspension. When we are asleep, our sensory nerves no longer perform their usual active duties, the action of the heart becomes slower, the brain is at rest, eliminating waste material and preparing for fresh activity when we awaken. Scientists believe that we dream principally because the suspension of activity is not complete. Thoughts come to our sleeping minds, causing images to flash into our mind's eye and it is these images that are the basis of our dreams.

Dreams are in some cases not simply thought out but actually acted by the dreamer. Such cases, sleep-walking for example, sleep-talking or the performance of acts during sleep of which the sleeper has no recollection on waking, are all phenomena of the sleeper's state of mind.

When we awaken and recall our dreams, we think that they have lasted for as long as we have been sleeping.

A-Z OF DREAMS

● ●

But when we are asleep time is suspended and what we dream of as an hour is a minute at most, and what seems like a few minutes is a mere second or two.

While we cannot control our dreams, we can take steps to improve the quality of our sleep – and without sleep there are no dreams.

First of all experiment with the length of time you spend asleep each night. As previously said, recent research suggests that seven hours is the optimum, but there can be no hard and fast rule for this. Vary the hours and see how different times affect you. If you are not working at your best, if you feel irritable and tired throughout the day, try sleeping a little more or a little less until you establish how long you should sleep for in order to give and feel your best every day.

Go to bed half an hour before you want to fall asleep. Read something light rather than thought-provoking, or simply spend thirty minutes calmly going through the day's events and planning tomorrow's or next week's.

What you eat and drink in the evening will affect the quality of your sleep. The old adage, 'breakfast like a prince, sup like a pauper', is excellent advice. If you go to bed with a full stomach, your digestion will be in

● ●

overdrive while you sleep. So avoid heavy evening meals, fatty foods and wind-producing ones such as raw vegetables, for several hours before going to bed. Similarly avoid caffeine and too much alcohol. Your grandmother was right when she made you a hot, milky bedtime drink when you went to stay with her. Some dreamers enjoy a tisane made with rosemary and sweetened with honey before going to bed.

Keep your bedroom as quiet and peaceful as possible. The modern trend for polished wooden floors and flimsy curtains does little to keep noise out. A pair of heavy curtains drawn across even an open window is excellent insulation. Decorate the room with colours that you find soothing, be they bright or brash, pastel or primary. Keep the lighting soft, using low watt pearl light bulbs rather than strong, clear-glass ones. If you prefer candlelight, take care: it may cast a lovely glow, but accidents can happen. So make sure the candles are snuffed before you get into bed.

And talking of beds, move yours north, south, east and west to find out which position encourages your best dreams. Many people who have styled their house in accordance with the principles of Feng Shui, the Chinese way of arranging furniture to ensure that energies are properly channelled within the house, report that they sleep more soundly and dream more vividly since they did so.

If your bedroom is too hot or too cold, the quality of your sleep will be adversely affected and if your bedclothes are too constricting you will find it difficult to sleep at all.

Herb-filled pillows encourage sleep and therefore dreams. There are many recipes, one of the most popular of which is mixing equal parts of lavender, sweet marjoram and rosemary with half parts of thyme and spearmint. To this mixture is added a tablespoon of orris root powder and a tablespoon of both dried orange peel and powdered cinnamon. The mixture is put into a flat, cotton or silk bag measuring 38cm x 31cm which is placed under the pillow, slightly to one side to allow the warmth of the sleeper's head to release the herbs' fragrances.

Many dreamers find that crystals help them sleep and stimulate their dreams, either placed under the pillow, under the bed, around it or on a bedside table. Their users believe that clear, sparkling crystals energize while opaque ones soothe and calm. Different stones have different qualities: rose quartz, for example, induces sleep, amethyst absorbs emotional trauma while luvulite encourages intuition.

Avoid, if possible, taking sleeping pills. They may help us find sleep when all else fails, but they appear to suppress the REM sleep during which we dream our dreams.

To get a good night's sleep, it is essential to leave the day behind. In reviewing the day's events, some people find it comforting to forgive themselves for an action they regret and in doing so develop a sense of calm that replaces any agitation they may have been experiencing.

Anyone who is having trouble sleeping (and there can be very few of us to whom that does not apply occasionally) may find relaxation techniques useful. One popular one is lie in bed, breathing in deeply through the nose and exhaling slowly through the mouth. While doing this, tighten the toes and let go three times. This time tighten and relax the muscles in the ankles three times, then do the same with the calves and thighs before tightening and relaxing both legs from toe to hip three times. Now do the same with the other parts of your body – buttocks, stomach,

● ●

spine, neck, hands and arms, face and scalp. By the time you have completed the process you should find you are so relaxed that sleep comes easily.

Other occasional insomniacs find that meditation breaks the non-sleep cycle. Many people are put off by the very word, imagining meditation to be the practice of cranks, sitting cross-legged on the floor, chanting weird words and thinking mystical thoughts. They are wrong to do so. Meditation lulls the mind into peaceful calm by focusing on a simple, continuing sensation – the tinkling of a fountain, the sound of waves lapping on a beach, the repetition of a soothing word or phrase. In doing this other thoughts and anxieties are crowded out, encouraging the peace of mind that is essential to a good night's sleep. There are countless books explaining the many meditation techniques, and tapes that play suitable sounds to encourage the meditative state.

If you are going to record your dreams in a Dream Diary, make sure that you have everything you need – pen or pencil, paper and torch – to hand. When you awake with a dream on your mind, write down the details immediately. If you have to rummage for pen and paper or get out of bed to put the light on, the details of your dream are likely to evaporate as you do so. Some dreamers dictate their dreams into tape-recorders as soon as they awaken. This is fine for those who sleep alone, irritating for those who share their bed with another, which is another reason for using a torch rather than switching on the bedside light, something that may awaken a slumbering partner.

Above all, be positive. Say to yourself, 'I am going to dream and I am going to remember my dreams when I wake up.' It is astonishing how many people report that going to bed in this positive frame of mind works. As Soozi Holbeche, one expert on dreams and dreaming writes, 'If you expect to dream with joy, pleasure and delight – you will.'

Different Types of Dream

Compensatory Dreams

Jung, the Swiss psychologist who coined the phrase 'collective consciousness' and applied it to dream analysis, believed that the purpose of dreaming is to restore psychological balance by producing material that subtly re-establishes total psychic equilibrium. Compensatory dreams do this, balancing us emotionally by encouraging us to express aspects of our personalities we cannot or will not express while we are awake. By showing us the opposite side of ourselves we can come to understand what we really are. A compensatory dream may show an aggressively ambitious dreamer being bullied by his colleagues and may encourage him or her to be less aggressive and more concerned for the feelings of fellow workers.

Diagnostic Dreams

Many medical men now ask their patients to describe their dreams as part of their consultations and use what they hear as part of their diagnoses. Traditional doctors may scoff at this, but there are well-documented examples that suggest dreams can play

● ●

a part in medicine. One such is the case of an American nurse whose doctors were baffled by her symptoms. One night she dreamed of a shellfish that opened to reveal a worm wriggling inside. An elderly woman then materialized, pointed at the worm and said, 'That's what's wrong with you.' The patient awakened and, being a nurse, was aware that eating contaminated shellfish can cause liver disease. She was later diagnosed as suffering from Hepatitis A.

Healing Dreams

Some healing dreams tell the dreamer what to do to cure whatever it is that ails us. Others may be trying to help our inner selves come to terms with their illnesses. Going to bed sick and waking up well, having experienced a healing dream may sound miraculous, but there are people who claim this has happened to them. Cases have occurred from Classical Greek to modern times. An inscription at Epidaurus on mainland Greece tells of a crippled girl who asked a friend to pray for her at the temple there. That night, she dreamed that Asklepeios, the Greek god of healing, appeared to her and asked why she hadn't been in the temple. When the girl replied that she was paralysed, the god replied, 'I will heal you here.' When the girl awoke in the morning, she was quite able to walk. Pie in the sky? Who can say.

DIFFERENT TYPES OF DREAM

Lucid Dreams

Some lucky dreamers are not only aware that they are dreaming, they somehow succeed in controlling their dreams in much the same way as a film director controls the action and his (or her) editor is responsible for what the film-goers eventually see. Some experts teach their followers techniques to help them do this, believing that lucid dreaming helps us to reach a higher state of consciousness and unlocks innate potential of which we are unaware. But others argue that controlling dreams is counter productive. The main purpose of dreams, they say, is to teach us something or to come to terms with some unsatisfactory aspect of our lives. By putting ourselves in the director's chair or the editing suite, we deprive our dreams of their self-will, repressing the part of our subconscious that is trying to help us help ourselves.

Nightmares

'Pray give me leave to ramble abroad with the Nightmare,' says the son of Hecate in Thomas Middleton's play, *The Witch*. 'For I have a great mind to overlay the parson's daughter.'

A hundred years later, during the eighteenth century, the Brothers Grimm, described them as travellers in disguise, ferried across a river to flood into the unsuspecting sleepers' minds.

Hundreds of years ago, in Old Japan, evil dreams were believed to be the result of evil spirits and a hideous creature with a lion's face, horse's body, tail of a cow, forelock of a rhinoceros and the feet of a tiger, called Baku. Anyone waking from a nightmare called upon Baku to eat the bad dream so that it would never return.

A nightmare is an extremely distressing dream, usually so distressing and terrifying that the sufferer wakes up suddenly, the events of the dream fresh in his or her mind. They tend to occur after several hours of sleep and, despite the widespread belief to the contrary, it is uncommon to find the dreamer thrashing around in bed, screaming or crying out during his or her bad dream.

Nightmares are often claustrophobic, the sufferer feeling threatened with a menacing, unseen presence in a confined space. Sometimes they take melodramatic form, maybe being forced into doing something terrible against the dreamer's will, or being led to the execution chamber, desperately protesting innocence. Another common nightmare is a feeling of falling into a bottomless pit: the old belief that if the pit is not bottomless and the dreamer crashes into it, then he or she dies instantly, has never been proved. How could it?

They are different from the night terrors that affect many children up to the age of puberty. Night terrors occur during the first two or three hours of sleep, with the sleeper thrashing about, screaming, whimpering or crying out for help.

It is unusual to have to be awakened from a nightmare. They are so vividly horrifying that they terrorize us into consciousness – or at least half-consciousness. It is difficult, on the other hand to waken a child whose thrashings and cries warn a parent of the night terrors.

People who wake from nightmares are usually able to recount in great detail what they have been dreaming. Children awoken after night terrors usually remember nothing of their dreams: all they recall is an overwhelming sense of fear.

Children who suffer from night terrors may wet the bed and may also sleepwalk. Adults who wake from a nightmare tend to go back to sleep, although it may be difficult for them to do so.

A-Z OF DREAMS

No one is quite sure what causes nightmares. Some people believe that they can be brought about by alcohol, drugs and medications (or the unsupervised withdrawal from them) or by some fever-inducing illnesses. Many people experience nightmares after having gone through a trauma of some sort, surgery maybe or the death of a loved one. Soldiers and veterans of military conflict often experience nightmares, and firemen, policemen and others involved in major accidents. Usually their dreams are directly related to their experiences.

Others report an increase in the incidence of nightmares when they are undergoing stress in their working lives, difficulty in their relationships, perhaps, or financial difficulties. Some mothers report that they experience nightmares more frequently during their pregnancies than before and after. (One study showed that the more nightmares a woman had while pregnant, the shorter her time in labour.)

An in-depth study in the United States showed that artists, musicians, writers and other artistic people tend to have more nightmares than those of a less-creative bent.

DIFFERENT TYPES OF DREAM

● ●

Some people become so concerned about nightmares, especially recurring ones, that they seek expert assistance. This is not usually necessary, unless there is an underlying drug habit. It may be useful to encourage children to talk about their nightmares with their parents or teachers, but again medical help is not usually necessary.

Adult nightmares can offer an excellent opportunity for self-exploration and understanding. As with other dreams, the dreamer can learn to decode the nightmare, its visual and symbolic language, and use it to understand relationships between the dream world and the waking one, and this is best done some time after the nightmare rather than in its immediate aftermath There are many aids to doing this. Writing the details down often helps, as does drawing or painting the images, using them as the basis for a poem or a piece of creative writing.

Some psychologists teach patients who suffer from recurring nightmares to master lucid dream techniques so that they can control their bad dreams and come to terms with them. Others claim that this ignores the reason why the patient is having nightmares in the first place and does more harm than good.

A-Z OF DREAMS

● ●

Physical Dreams

Such dreams are normally anxiety-induced, superimposed on the sleeping mind by the conscious. Drug induced dreams are physical, as are dreams brought about by ill-health and fever. Most dream analysts pay little heed to physical dreams, believing them to have little significance.

Prescient Dreams

Dream analysts believe that all dreams possess an element of warning or prescience, some more than others. What some people call prescient dreams, others call prophetic, precognitive or telepathic. These are the dreams that people less sophisticated than world-weary westerners believe can guide, warn and inform. Genghis Khan is said to have dreamed what fate held in store for him: centuries later Jung claimed to have had several prophetic dreams about the Second World War.

Prophetic dreams, like Jung's, are usually concerned with the future and with events more impersonal than personal, affecting the community at large rather than just the dreamer. Precognitive dreams, on the other hand, are much more personal, advising the dreamer not to do something. Would-be travellers to the United States who shunned the *Titanic* on its fateful maiden

● ●

voyage in 1912, because they had warning dreams, could be said to have experienced dreams that were both precognitive, warning them not to embark, and prophetic in that they affected many more people than just themselves.

Telepathic, or clairvoyant, dreams are those that provide us with information about events of which we are completely unaware consciously. Several years ago, Belgian police faced public ridicule when they heeded the advice of a telepathic dreamer who contacted them during a missing-person investigation. It was the sceptics who were proved wrong for when they did as the dreamer bid, the police found the body of the missing person, someone with whom the dreamer had no connection or knowledge of whatsoever.

Prodromic Dreams

The word 'prodromic' comes from the Greek 'prodromos' meaning 'forerunner' and means any symptom that signals the impending onset of a disease and, like healing dreams they warn of impending ill-health. They are often nightmarish, featuring wars, fire or natural disasters, or they can be intensely personal.

A-Z OF DREAMS

● ●

Recurring Dreams

A dream that comes back time and time again, obviously has special significance. Many dream experts regard them as messages from the inner self trying to awaken us to a problem or perhaps feeling which we have subconsciously been ignoring or refusing to deal with. The very fact that the dream recurs, either frightening, shocking perhaps even amusing us, forces us to pay attention to it. By pointing out our unconscious frustrations, resentments or whatever is wrong in our lives, the dream releases repressed emotional energy and once we acknowledge this, it forces us to analyse the dream and take the appropriate action.

Sexual Dreams

Sex features in everyone's dreams at some time in their lives. Some people, often those who are inhibited, repressed or uncomfortable with their sexuality, wake up feeling guilty at the pleasure they have experienced indulging in sexual activities that would shame them in their waking lives. If the dreamer is a pubescent schoolboy whose dreams culminate in orgasm, it should be explained to him that what has happened is part of the growing-up process and is nothing to be ashamed of. Adults who feel ashamed of dreaming of

• •

sexual activity should also be reassured that there is nothing to be ashamed of.

Research seems to suggest that both men and women whose sexual dreams cause embarrassment or guilt, are the kind of people who repress and ignore problems, and not just sexual problems, in their waking lives. It also points to the fact that those who are quite unembarrassed by sexual dreams tend to be far more creative than those who clam up when asked to talk about them.

Sexual dreams do have a part to play in loosening our attitude to sex and sexuality: they also, according to some experts, symbolize union with various aspects of ourselves. If we dream of engaging in sexual activity with someone we know, our subconscious is simply encouraging us to recognize qualities in that person that we admire and telling us that we should try and merge these aspects into our own personalities. If we dream of sexual play with a member of our own sex, our subconscious is not telling as that we are latently homosexual, it is merely encouraging us to keep in touch with the feminine side or masculine side of our personalities, depending on the sex of the sleeper.

A-Z OF DREAMS

●●●●●●●●●●●●●●●●●●●●●●●●●●●●●●●●●●●●

Shadow Dreams

Aspects of ourselves that we find unpleasant and unacceptable are often called our shadow personalities. Things we dislike in others, are often things we subconsciously acknowledge in ourselves. In dreams this can manifest itself in seeing ourselves as others see us: and if we can accept that what we have dreamed is a truer picture of ourselves than the one we consciously have, then we can learn from these dreams and become nicer people.

Keeping a Dream Diary

There can be very few of us who have not awoken convinced that we have enjoyed a dreamless sleep only, a few hours later, to experience a flash of a memory about something we **did** dream and for that fragment to expand into a memory of a complete dream.

For those of us who want to use our dreams to help us understand more of ourselves and our relationships and interactions with others this is not a satisfactory state of affairs. We must find a way of holding on to our dreams when we awaken and record them.

To this end, it is best either to keep a pencil and pad by the bedside to write down details of what has been dreamed, or a cassette-recorder into which what has been dreamt can be dictated.

But before a word is written or a sentence spoken, the details of the dream have to be recalled, something which is not always easy. Talking aloud can help bring back details of a dream. One detail leads to another and another and soon a whole picture is built up.

A-Z OF DREAMS

● ●

Some people find it helpful to say as they get into bed,
'I am going to dream tonight, and I will remember what
I dream when I wake up.' Frederic Perls, the
psychologist who believed in the gestalt theory of
dream interpretation, prompted his patients to recall
details of their dreams by telling them to 'ask' their
dream why it was making it difficult for the dreamer to
remember. Surprisingly, it worked for the majority.

Most people who keep a dream diary use the bedside
notebook or cassette as a prompt. When they
awaken, they lie for a moment or two collecting their
thoughts, before reaching for pad or machine. They
don't try to record every detail at this stage, that's for
later. They simply note down a few words that they
know will bring back full details later when they come
to write up their dream diary.

The journal in which details of dreams dreamt and
interpreted should be large enough to allow a two-
page spread to be devoted to each dream. The first
thing to write down is the date, which should go at the
top of the left-hand page. Beneath this, the general
atmosphere of the dream should be recorded – happy
or sad, funny or serious, relaxing or frightening. Noting
the atmosphere is normally a useful aid to interpreting
the dream as the pervading atmosphere is a pointer to

the emotional state of the dreamer and his or her
feelings about problems that have been recently
overcome, are presently being faced or are looming
on the horizon.

Beneath this, any colour that seemed to dominate the
dream should be noted. Some people dream mainly
in black and white, others as glorious technicolour.
When a colour does dominate it should be considered
as a separate symbol. Red indicates anger, yellow
and orange usually accompany a happy dream and
are indicative of encouragement. Blue is often
indicative of nostalgia and green is often the dominant
colour when a dreamer is experiencing feelings of
envy of others or dissatisfaction with something in his
or her life. Black often points to depression, while
white is a sign of hope.

Some dream journalists devote a line or two to writing
down what they thought may have triggered the dream
– a discussion with a colleague about a job promotion,
a row with a spouse about the housekeeping budget,
a call from a child's school, whatever.

The rest of the left-hand page is devoted to a narrative
of how the dream unfolded. It's the content that's
important, not the style. Anyone worried that his or her

A-Z OF DREAMS

● ●

literary style would not stand up to critical scrutiny need not worry. Even if the journal is to be read by others as part of a group exercise in dream interpretation, it's the dream that counts, not skill (or lack of it) with which the words have been written!

Put in as much detail as possible. One expert suggests before the complete narrative is committed to paper or tape, a short, bullet-point summary should be written down, giving the dream a title and noting the action, the feelings experienced (both during the dream and on awakening), the setting, the people and the symbols. These bullet-points can all be used as aides-mémoire if writing the complete narrative has to wait until later in the day.

The right-hand page should be devoted to interpreting what has been dreamt.

Some people find it useful to work in groups that meet regularly to discuss and analyse each member's dream. Obviously, it is essential that dreams have to be recorded in considerable detail for this to work successfully. A tiny fragment that has been overlooked by one dreamer in his or her dream journal may have proved to be the trigger for another member to provide an accurate insight into the dream.

● ●

Meeting more than once a fortnight does not give each member the chance to have thought thoroughly about the dream they want to discuss. Meeting at intervals of longer than once a month is too long: even with the prompt that a well-kept dream journal provides, clarity may have been clouded by subsequent dreams.

Members must be frank in relating details of their dreams, and their minds must be open to the suggestions of others.

Sweet dreams!

A Houseful of Dreams

Buildings play a large part in our lives and an equally large part in our dreams. Many interpreters believe that in our dreams they represent the structure that we aim to give to our waking lives. And as we often form our judgements of people we meet (in part if not in full) from the environments in which they live and work, these features influence the environment of the dreams themselves. For example a house with doors and windows flung open may represent someone we know who has an open, extrovert personality and that is the thing that comes to mind when we first think of them. Similarly, a house with windows and doors firmly closed may indicate that we think of the person it represents as being shy and introverted, uncommunicative and taciturn. And just as the buildings themselves have their own interpretations, so do the fixtures and fittings within.

Attics relate to the past and often indicate that the dreamer feels that he has failed to achieve what was expected of him when he was younger – the pressures of parental expectation can burden us long after our mothers and fathers have died.

A-Z OF DREAMS

● ●

Basements and cellars are thought to represent the subconscious. When they appear in our dreams they are a signal that because we have been unable to handle things or face up to them in an adult way, we have put them to the back of our minds where they are starting to fester in some way. To dream that you are in a cold, damp cellar indicates that you are plagued with doubts. All self-confidence may well be about to evaporate like steam from a boiling kettle and you will be sunk into a deep depression from which you will find it hard to escape unless you can somehow, to put it bluntly, get a grip. Dreams of a cellar can also portend loss of property. When dreamers dream of a cellar filled with wine and stores, there is a fair chance that they will be offered a share in the profits of some sort of business venture. Before saying, 'Yes!' remember that all that glistens is not gold! Do your homework, especially into the background of whoever is putting the deal together: it may be distinctly shady! For a woman to have a similar dream is an indication that she may be about to receive an offer of marriage – from someone who is a reckless gambler!

● ●

Bathrooms, when they feature in the dream house, often have one very obvious meaning – the body is trying to warn the dreamer that it's time to get up and go to the loo! Very often if the dreamer sees himself (and research has shown that it is more likely to be a male) passing water in his dreams, he has had a nasty accident! On a broader level, when we dream of bathrooms our subconscious is trying to tell us that there is something regarding matters of personal cleanliness that is niggling us. But for a young woman to dream of bathrooms is an indication that she is being increasingly seen as frivolous and flighty! There is one curious dream that has been dreamt by several sleepers who have reported seeing roses in the dream bathroom. The interpretation put on this by a noted interpreter is that if the flowers are white, then sickness may be about to visit the dreamer.

Baths have a variety of meanings depending on the sex of the dreamer and the temperature of the water! If seen by a young woman she may well be increasingly afraid that other people are working against her in some way, their aim being to cause others to see her in a bad light. If the dreamer is pregnant, she should take special care, as the dream has been associated with miscarrying the baby. If the dreamer is a woman who is still in mourning for a husband who died some time before, she is being told that it is time to move on: get out more and look for new love. For a man to dream that he is in the tub is a warning that, if he is not careful, he may find himself accused of being unfaithful. Perversely, if the water is warm and relaxing, then bad things are in the offing: but if it is cold, then good health is forecast and good news is on the way. If the dreamer is sharing a bath, acquaintances may turn out to be false friends – especially if the water is not clean.

Bedrooms are the places where we relax most and where most people indulge in sexual activities. To see them in a dream is an indication that we have been working too hard and need to find more time to indulge our private passions. If the linen on the bed has been freshly laundered, worries are about to fly out of the window. If the dreamer is a woman and she sees such a bed, a new lover may be about to make himself known to her. A dreamer who sees him or herself in bed in a room that is unfamiliar, is being forewarned that friends who have not been around for some time may be about to make an unexpected and unannounced visit. For a sick person to dream of being in bed is a bad omen. Things might be about to get worse before they get better – if they ever do! Dreamers who see themselves asleep in an al fresco bed of some sort are being prewarned that good fortune is about to smile and make life extremely delightful.

Chairs tell the dreamer that there is an obligation that is due to be met but for some reason there is a reluctance on the dreamer's part to do this. But if the right action is not taken and duties fulfilled as promised, a significant loss may result. To dream of a friend sitting quite motionless on a chair is a sign that he or she might be about to be hit by a bout of ill health – and it could be serious.

Chandeliers, if they are in sparkling condition, tell the dreamer to set his sights high for what seems absolutely unobtainable at present is there for the taking if he puts his mind to it. On the other hand, if the chandelier is broken or in need of a good clean, then beware of investing in a speculative venture. It will end not just in tears but in significant financial loss. And if the lights flicker and go out, what seems to be a promising future will be clouded by disappointment.

Chapels may be soothing places to visit, but when they feature in dreams they warn of a fall in social standing and that business dealings may be about to nosedive. To be in a chapel suggests that disappointment is in the offing. If young people see

● ●

themselves going into a chapel, someone who promises true love is speaking falsely and should be ignored.

Churches and other religious buildings suggest that we are seeking sanctuary, a place where we may find the serenity to be at peace with ourselves. They also portend that in our everyday lives, we are seeking to iron out imperfections and make ourselves better, more spiritual people. If the church is in the distance, a long looked-forward-to event will turn out to be a huge disappointment.

Churchyards can be good news or bad. Seen in spring, with flowers budding and about to burst into bloom, suggests that travel to pleasant places is on the cards, and even better, the trip will be in the convivial company of good friends. On the other hand, if the churchyard is seen in winter, separation from home and friends is likely, and poverty may be about to rear its unwelcome head! For someone young and in love to dream of a churchyard, regardless of the weather, is to be told that he or she will never marry their current lover, but that they will find true love and happiness with someone else. And the nice thing is that so will the current boy- or girl-friend.

Cisterns may not spring to mind when one thinks of the things one dreams of. But there is no apparent logic in the language of dreams, and cisterns do have their own significance to the dreamer. They can mean that the seeds of disappointment have been sown in the minds of the dreamer's friends and that they are starting to see him or her as someone who is taking advantage of the friendship. For a dreamer to see that he or she is drawing water from a cistern is also a warning. This time, that in seeking enjoyment and pleasure, the dreamer is secretly worried that the limits of propriety are in danger of being broken. Even worse is to see an empty cistern for it serves as a warning that today's happiness contains the seeds of tomorrow's sorrows.

Cookers, be they gas, electric or the venerable Aga, suggests that the dreamer's intervention in what could be an unpleasant situation will stop it developing into such, and that as a result, friendships will be strengthened. If the dreamer is woman, she is warned not to be seen to be too keen to get into someone's romantic good books, or else a close friendship with a third party could be broken for ever.

A-Z OF DREAMS

Cots predict that an affliction of some sort – sickness or illness – is about to strike the dreamer. If the cots are lined up hospital fashion in a neat row, then the dreamer will not be alone in being ill.

Couches, when seen with the dreamer lounging on them, say that hopes may take wing but that they will crash land almost as soon as they have taken off! They warn the dreamer to be especially careful in business matters for if there is the slightest loss of concentration, the effect could be out of all proportion to the cause.

Cradles dreamt of occupied by a bonny baby tell the dreamer that if things turn out as planned, prosperity is theirs for the taking and that if they have children, the offspring will do their parents proud and stay friends with them throughout their lives. But if a young mother sees herself rocking her own baby in a cradle, another member of the family could be about to come down with an illness of some sort. If a childless, unmarried woman dreams that she is rocking a cradle she should keep her ears open for tittle-tattle that may be being spread about her.

Decorating a house suggests that the dreamer is increasingly aware that personal relationships have fallen into disrepair and that fences need to be mended.

●●●●●●●●●●●●●●●●●●●●●●●●●●●●●●●●●●●

Desks seen being used by dreamers suggest that bad luck may roll down on them. But if there are coins or banknotes on the surface, then dreamers who have been having financial problems may find that an unexpected windfall, maybe in the form of a bonus or a win of some sort, is about to help ease things.

Domes, despite their recent reputation as being something of a white elephant (to Britain's Labour Party, at least), herald good news and bad – it all depends if the dreamer sees him or herself as being inside or seeing one from a distance. If you are in the dome of a building, then fate has good things in store for you, and you will grow to become widely respected by people who you don't at present know. On the other hand, if you see one from far away, you will be lucky even to reach the foothills in climbing the mountain of your ambition. And if you have set your amorous sights on someone, then think again and cast your eyes elsewhere for he or she will dismiss your advances out of hand.

Doorbells heard or being rung in a dream warn that your routine is about to be abruptly disrupted by a summons to attend to an urgent business matter or to the bedside of an ailing relative.

A-Z OF DREAMS

● ●

Doors have many rneanings in the dream dictionary.
Many psychologists believe that they represent the
body's openings, and therefore the dreamer's
sexuality. Opening and closing doors can indicate the
dreamer's attitude to sex and sexuality, while refusing
to open a door can be symptomatic of a childish
approach to sex. To be seen barring a door suggests
that the dreamer is searching for self-protection.
Dreaming of doors can suggest that the dreamer is
willing to present a more approachable face to society.
But it can also suggest that in appearing more
approachable, the dreamer might be worried that he
or she will appear to be seen as being more vulnerable
and that others may take advantage of this. To dream
of breaking a door down, tells the dreamer that now is
the time to tackle any inhibitions that have been
holding him back, especially in sexual matters. To
dream of going through one suggests that you are
trying to escape the slanders that vituperative tongues
are casting in your direction. There is an exception: if
the door you are entering is one that you remember
from your childhood home, then good times are on the
other side. Dreaming of coming out of the rain and
going through a door at night suggests, to a female
dreamer, that she has been up to something of which
she is deeply ashamed. To a male, the same dream
signifies that he is about to have to draw on his

resources to pay for his (as yet unknown) vices! To see others going through a door tells the dreamer that he or she is going to have to work extremely hard to straighten out their financial affairs. To see a door fall off its hinges and injure someone after you have been trying to close it is a warning that some advice you have given him or her will cause them unhappiness or bad luck. To see someone try to lock a door and then to see it become unhinged says that you will hear that a friend has or is about to come unstuck in some way and that you are or will be powerless to help them.

Elevators going up suggest that the dreamer's luck will rise. And conversely, if it's going down, then luck is likely to go in a similar direction. It's lucky to see yourself missing an elevator that's going down, though, for then you will escape disappointment that will hit others. To see one going neither up nor down, says that danger in some guise or other is imminent. On a less practical level, a descending lift suggests that the dreamer is willing to delve deep into his or her subconscious to make themselves more complete people. On the other hand, to see themselves going up in a lift suggest that the dreamer believes that it is in the spiritual rather than the practical that solutions to problems lie.

A-Z OF DREAMS

● ●

Halls and vestibules are an indication that we are
concerned with the way in which we meet and relate
to other people. Depending on the circumstances and
the way the dreamer sees himself, halls can be a sign
that the dreamer is being too private in his dealings
with others, or that he is being too open. Only he can
know which is which.

Hotels and other temporary residences may tell
dreamers that they are becoming increasingly aware
of insecurities that are causing others to question
their abilities.

Houses are almost always a reference to the soul
and that which attempts to give structure to our
spiritual and corporeal lives. If the dream house is
shared with another person, then the dreamer may be
feeling threatened by an aspect of his personality that
he has long kept hidden but that is threatening to
make itself public. If different parts of the house are
being used for different purposes, then the dreamer is
becoming increasingly aware of an inner conflict
between two aspects of his personality that is making
him feel uneasy. The front of the house is thought by
interpreters to represent the face we present to the
world. Entering or leaving the house is, it is thought, the
psyche's way of telling the dreamer that a certain

situation should be faced in an introvert or extrovert fashion respectively.

Igloos are not unique to the dreams of Inuits to whom they are familiar. The igloo's shape suggests that it is a symbol of sanctuary and of being whole, and when they appear in dreams, they indicate, perhaps, a need to escape from the pressures of everyday life, maybe to search for something that we hope would make us better, more rounded people.

Kitchens warn that the dreamer is about to come face to face with an emergency of some sort which he or she will find extremely distressing. If the dreamer is a woman and her dream kitchen is spick and span, good things lie in store for her.

Libraries, being the rooms (albeit it in grander houses) where books and by implication knowledge are stored are often taken as being symbolic of our minds and how we store and cope with the information we receive.

Mansions and good fortune go hand in hand and to dream of being in one suggests that the dreamer will never go hungry and will never know the feeling that there is too much month at the end of a salary cheque! To see a mansion in the distance portends that the good life beckons but not in the immediate future. There is one curious exception to the good fortune that mansions herald. If, and it has been reported, someone dreams of being in a haunted mansion, then some unexpected misfortune will shatter the dreamer's present contentment.

Moving house tells that the dreamer has an as yet unspoken desire for change. If the house is a larger one than the one at present lived in, that's indicative of a desire to live a more open life. If the house is smaller, then the dreamer may be feeling a need to unburden him or herself of something that has been gnawing away at him or her for some time.

Pyramids suggest that change is in the offing – not one or two changes, but a whole barrowload of them. To see yourself climbing a pyramid means you have quite a journey ahead of you before you get what you want out of life. If it is a woman who has this dream, then she is warned that the man she plans to marry is not the one for her.

Rooms are often regarded as dream symbols of various parts of our personalities or levels of comprehension. Each room has its own significance for the dreamer and many of those are listed separately in this section. But in general they are often taken as symbolizing the womb and the mother figure. According to lore, if they are richly furnished, they herald an upturn in fortunes. It might be in the form of a legacy or it might be that a gamble pays off in spades. For a young woman to dream of such a room is a sign that someone who at the moment is simply an acquaintance may be about to feature more significantly – very significantly in her romantic life and will eventually keep her in some considerable style. If the room is plainly furnished, then romance will bloom, but the suitor, while ardent, will be comfortably off rather than wealthy.

Stairs and staircases often feature in the dreams of those who are aware that there are certain steps that have to be taken before goals are achieved. Climbing the stairs suggests that the goal may be a spiritual one. Going down a set of stairs, curiously, suggests that the dreamer is concerned that their sexual techniques might not be keeping their partners happy! To dream of falling down stairs is a sign that others are seeing you with envy, or worse, hatred in their eyes. Seeing others descend a staircase, warns dreamers to enjoy the good times while they can, for there are a few squalls on the horizon.

A-Z OF DREAMS

●●●

Walls can be good and they can be bad. If the dreamer sees one block the way ahead, then losses are signified in business dealings probably brought about by listening to well-meaning but ill-informed advice. To see yourself jumping over a wall means that obstacles that present themselves will be cleared, while to break through one, you will achieve your ambitions but only after a long, hard slog. Knocking a wall down, suggests that enemies had better look out, for you have the scent of victory in your nostrils and are not to be beaten. A young woman who dreams that she is walking along the top of a wall is being given advance notice that plans she is laying down to secure her future happiness are well founded. But if she dreams that she is hiding behind a wall, then she has probably formed an attachment with someone she would rather the world did not find out about.

Windows warn that in some aspect of life that the dreamer holds dear, hope is about to be replaced by despair. And no matter how much effort is put in to restore things to what they were, it will take some time for that to happen, if indeed it ever does. If the windows are closed, then someone close to the dreamer may be about to jump ship! And if the glass is broken, then people you love might be about to accuse you of disloyalty.

A Mineful of Dreams

Agate may be a semi-precious stone, but its meaning is far from precious to the dreamer. It signifies three s's – sadness, sickness and setbacks.

Alabaster is a sign of success in marriage and in any legal disputes. But if the dream ends with a piece of figure cast from this cool, elegant stone dropped and broken, then sorrow looms and the dreamers will be called upon to repent of something done in the distant past. If the dreamer is a young woman and she sees herself opening an alabaster box then some careless action will result in the loss of something she holds dear – property perhaps, her lover maybe or even worse – her reputation.

Aluminium is a metal that can glow warmly but become easily tarnished. Dreamed of in its former state suggests that the dreamer will glow with contentment no matter how healthy the state of the bank balance. Seen in the latter state, especially by a woman, then life will be dulled by unexpected sorrow and loss.

A-Z OF DREAMS

Amethyst is good news for businessmen, bad news for young women who have recently become engaged. To the former it is full order books and excellent sales; to the latter it warns that the engagement will be broken off.

Anvils are not something that feature much in the current consciousness. But if one does get hammered into your sleep it signifies either new life, or that something that lies latent or in immature form within you is about to come to the surface to be made into a new shape.

Armour, as worn by knights of old, indicates that the sleeper seeks protection from something that is threatening him or her. Or it can confirm an increasing awareness that there is something rigid in the personality – something inflexible that is preventing a move into a new situation.

Axes are often regarded as symbols of time. Their association with the Norse god of thunder, Thor, also lend them associations with power and force. If they are seen in a dream, they point to an awareness that in order to extricate ourselves from a troubling situation, we need to take some sort of action that will destroy something we hold dear – a friendship perhaps, or a business relationship.

Bayonets rarely feature in the dreams of non-military types, but they were common in days when these weapons were standard issue to the armed forces. A broken bayonet was an ill omen, foretelling as it did disgrace in the offing: an officer may face being returned to the ranks; a private soldier may be about to be dishonourably discharged. But if the bayonet was glinting brightly, then the dreamer was being given the good news that he was gaining the confidence of his superiors and would gain promotion. A bayonet dreamed of as being used in battle, was interpreted as heralding a long period of peace! On the rare occasions when a bayonet does feature in the dreams of a contemporary dreamer, similar interpretations can be laid on them.

A **bell** tolling its way into a dream, was traditionally taken as a warning of impending disaster or the death of someone close. The peals alert the sleeper to potential mistakes – perhaps the subconscious knowledge that a task recently fulfilled has not been done one hundred percent effectively and the consequences of this could cause danger. Bells also tell that whoever hears them in their dreams is insecure and is desperately seeking the approval of others.

Blacksmiths at work in your dreams, indicate that the dreamer may well be hammered by trouble on the horizon, particularly as the result of a lawsuit.

Bottles have a variety of symbolic meanings in the litany of dreams: a baby's feeding bottle points to a need to be nurtured before the dreamer's full potential can be realized. A bottle of alcohol in any form can show that there is a desire to celebrate something that has been overlooked: conversely it can warn the dreamer that there has been a little too much celebration recently and the body would like a chance to get back into balance. If the bottle is broken, it could warn that someone is about to turn to aggression to get his or her own way, or that a hoped-for success will turn out to end in failure.

Brass objects dreamed of denote climbing the ladder of professional success more rapidly than you hoped to do. But while each rung on the ladder is strong, you may fear putting your weight on it in case it gives way.

Bronze suggests that the road ahead is uncertain and that no matter what path is taken, fortune will tantalize but never quite come within reach. If a woman dreams of a bronze statue then the man she has set her heart on will not be hers, however hard she tries. And if it moves, it tells that she will be one of a passionate partnership, but that the flame of passion will die and will not be rekindled.

Buckets have a curiously precise meaning, at least those with the bottom knocked out do. For in the language of dreams, this suggests that a fraud of some kind will cost the dreamer dear unless he heeds the warning and takes the necessary precautions.

Buckles foretell that if the dreamer comes up against evil in any of its often attractive guises, he will find the strength to overcome it. Or if he is about to face a challenging situation, there will be no buckling under the pressure. To dream that a buckle is being fastened, shows that when responsibility is offered, it will be readily accepted.

Cauldrons probably bring to mind a picture of witches brewing magical potions. But to many people of the New Age, the cauldron is a symbol of the womb.

In the language of dreams such a receptacle signifies abundance and nourishment, fertility and sustenance. On a more spiritual level, to dream of a cauldron may be telling us that our intuitive abilities are bubbling away deep within us, unacknowledged, and that now is the time to do something about them.

Coal seen lighting our dreams with its bright flames suggests change of a pleasant nature is about to warm our lives. If the coal has turned to ash, then the change will be of a distinctly unpleasant nature. And if the coal is unlit, then there may be trouble of an unspecified nature looming. Soot and coal dust portend unhappiness in affairs of the heart and that those we love will be argumentative and generally irksome.

Coins are common features of all our lives and not surprisingly a common feature of many dreams. To dream of many coins indicates a life of plenty. Silver coins have a special significance for farmers for they foretell that the harvest will be no better than average. They also suggest a spell of fair weather is on the way. And it is a paradox that for a businessman to dream of gold coins forewarns of a downturn in cashflow and the prospect of a depression looming.

• •

Compasses set us in the right direction in our waking hours, and in our dreams, a compass or lodestone points to our search for new horizons and fresh activities. It may be that we have been offered such changes and are trying to decide to pick up the gauntlet of challenge and move on. Compasses can also tell that deep down we are feeling aggrieved about something and are seeking justice. Compasses that feature in a young person's dreams point to the fact that they will fall behind in their studies and that the midnight oil has to be burned if oncoming exams are to be passed with merit.

Copper warns that those in authority over us, who may have been perfectly pleasant in the past, may be about to change and act oppressively towards us.

Corkscrews, sadly, are symbolic that a close relative will suffer a long spell of illness that will give rise to deep anxiety. If, in the dream, the corkscrew breaks while it is being used, then be warned that a close friend will contract a serious infectious illness and may well die.

Crystals are unwelcome signs in dreams. They may brighten our waking lives but they darken our dreams

● ●

by signalling depression is in the offing as a result of a friendship coming to an end, or a business transaction ending in an unsatisfactory manner.

Cymbals ringing through our dreams indicate that we are aware that our lives have somehow gone out of kilter and that we are seeking to set the vibrations back to a settling rhythm and banish the discordance that we are going through.

Diamonds signify that those in positions of authority will smile at you and nudge you up the ladder of success at every opportunity. If a young woman dreams that an admirer is giving her diamonds then she should stick with him for he will do well and marriage to him would ensure a comfortable and prosperous life. But if the dream concerns losing diamonds then disgrace is waiting to welcome the dreamer in the not too distant future. That's what one source suggests. Others put different interpretations on dream diamonds. To pick up a dropped diamond may mean loss or sorrow, while to be offered one on a plate signifies wealth success and happiness. And another claims that wearing diamonds might indicate that the dreamer will be mixed up in some gossip that will lead to serious trouble, perhaps even loss of employment.

● ●

Earth is symbolic of the nurturing we all need at every stage as we move from birth to death. By the time we reach adulthood we have all established friendships and networks: to dream of earth now warns us that we may be taking these for granted and that they, too, need nurturing if they are to continue to sustain us. If the dreamer dreams that the earth is closing in and about to engulf him, it may presage that he feels overwhelmed by being nurtured too much.

Emeralds warn that others mentioned in a will might dispute an inheritance. A young man who dreams that his fiancée is wearing these lustrous, green stones is being warned that love is not enough for her: she wants wealth and will break off the engagement if a more prosperous suitor comes along. Dreaming of buying an emerald warns that money could be about to get a bit tight, and to take the necessary precautions. According to Romany folklore, a dream of emeralds indicates a rise in rank and a boost to the bank balance.

Fences, either metal or the more rustic wooden variety tell us of a deep awareness of the boundaries that are restricting us. This may indicate that the dreamer feels socially inferior to his friends and colleagues, or even that his or her spouse is setting boundaries to their relationship. But if we can get over the fence, these boundaries will be behind us – both in our dreams and in our waking lives, too.

Files use abrasion to form that which they are rubbed against. So it's hardly surprising that to dream of such a tool indicates that we are being too abrasive with friends and colleagues in our attempts to shape them to our will. Taking a softly, softly approach is just as likely to get us our own way as rubbing people up the wrong way.

Glass has many meanings for the dreamer. To see oneself looking through it warns that disappointment will dull one's life. But if it's a clear glass window that is being gazed through, then that interview you may have just had will result in a job offer – but a less important position than you hoped for. To see one's face in a looking glass is a sign that a spouse may be about to turn to another for love. If there is another face in the mirror alongside the dreamer's then he or she is leading a double life and is not just deceiving themselves, but their friends as well. Breaking a mirror is a sign that a fatal accident is on the cards. To drop and smash a glass dish is a sign that an enterprise in which you are involved will come to a sudden end. Handling a pane of glass suggests that there are uncertainties ahead in business: if the glass breaks

• •

then the uncertainty will end in failure. To dream of a glass house warns that a flatterer will cause injury, especially for a female dreamer who will find that the silver-tongued flatterer will damage her reputation.

Gold has mixed meanings in the symbolism of dreams. If it is being handled, then success at anything to which the dreamer turns his hand is within his grasp. And lucky in one way is the woman who dreams that she is given gold in any form for she will marry a wealthy man: but the luck may sour for his mercenary manner will irritate her with increasing intensity. To dream of finding gold objects suggests that your talents will shine so brightly that honours and wealth are prizes you will be awarded. But to dream of finding a gold vein indicates that the honours will not lie easily on the dreamer's head and the wealth will make him feel uncomfortable in some way. Gold lost in dreams indicates opportunities lost in real life – and lost through no one's fault but the dreamer's. And dreams of working in a gold mine forewarn that something in your life may start tongues wagging.

Gravel is not to be dreamed of by those seeking business success for it suggests that schemes and enterprises will not bear fruit. If there is dirt mixed with the gravel then beware of any speculative ventures

● ●

you may be invited to become involved in: the loss you incur could cost you property.

Handcuffs are a strong indication that the dreamer fears he is being restrained in some way. The restraint may be put in our paths by a someone who holds authority over us, or it may be our own doubts and fears that are holding us back, restraining us from reaching our true potential. A dreamer who dreams that he is putting handcuffs on someone he recognizes is acknowledging a desire to bind that person to him and that deep down there is a possessiveness in his feelings towards the person being handcuffed.

Iron is not a metal that dreamers should welcome into their dreams. See yourself struggling under the weight of this element and you will soon have to face the harsh realities of material loss. To hit someone with an iron bar warns that those dependent on you see you as selfish and cruel. To see yourself cast in the role of iron manufacturer suggests an unscrupulous nature that will stop at nothing to gain personal wealth. If you see yourself selling a piece of iron, then you are surrounding yourself with friends of a dubious nature. And to wind up this litany of iron's base meanings, to dream of old, rusty iron warns that poverty and disappointment litter the way ahead.

● ●

Lead points to disappointment in many directions. For a man, to dream of a lead mine warns that the docile girl he marries will turn out to be a deceitful shrew, and that business ventures will be viewed with suspicion by friends and colleagues alike. And to dream of molten lead forewarns that impatience will lead you and your friends down the path of failure.

Marble is a cold stone and to dream of a marble quarry tells that the dreamer may be warmed by financial success, but his life will be a chill one, devoid of any affection whatsoever. If the marble is being polished, an inheritance, not necessarily of a financial nature, but pleasing nonetheless, will soon be revealed. To dream of dropping a piece of marble and seeing it smash into pieces is a sign that disfavour brought on by a lapse of morals will soon cloud the dreamer's life.

Mercury indicates that someone is plotting against you and could cause you to have to make unhappy changes in your life. Featuring in female dreams, it warns that separation from her family, perhaps brought about by desertion, is about to bring the dreamer great unhappiness.

A-Z OF DREAMS

Minerals of an unspecified nature suggest that difficulties at present being experienced will be overcome and that sunshine is about to peek through the clouds that have been darkening the horizon. But, if the dream concerns walking over land that is being mined, then beware, for there is distress in the offing. It will pass, though, but it will have a lasting effect on your life.

Pearls suggest that the dreamer's social life is in for a boost and that those in trade are in for a spell of good business. A young, engaged woman who dreams that she is wearing a string of pearls is being told that she has been lucky in her choice of lover. But if she dreams that the string breaks and the pearls cascade to the floor, then bereavement is presaged – perhaps not someone particularly close, but linked closely enough to cause some distress. And if a young woman sees herself looking at another's pearls with envy in her eyes, then her ambition to marry well and acquire wealth will be such that others will find it off-putting. Romany folk believe that a dream of pearls is a dream of tears, especially for brides.

Pewter is a metal that was once widely used but fell out of favour. Even so, it is still significant to the dreamer as it warns that circumstances may start to become straitened in the not too distant future.

● ●

Powder warns you to look carefully among your business associates for someone who seems to be on your side, but who will use unscrupulous methods to get his or her own way – even if it means stabbing the dreamer in the back.

Quarries have two meanings in the dream dictionary. If they are being worked, take heart, for you will achieve your aims by hard work. If the quarry is idle, then you may be about to experience failure or disappointment.

Rhinestones may glitter and dazzle but they soon lose their shine. It is appropriate therefore that one of their dream meanings is that forthcoming pleasures will not last long. If, in the course of the dream, the rhinestone makes a miraculous transformation to the real thing, then what was thought to have been a trifling insignificant act may turn out to have undreamed of and happy consequences.

Rocks, in general when they feature in dreams, are not a particularly welcome symbol for they indicate that the way ahead will be fraught with reversal, that relationships will run into disharmony and that the outlook is not a happy one. If you see yourself walking over ore-bearing rocks business success will come to you, but only after you have explored several avenues and come to dead ends each time.

• •

Rubies, like amethyst, are good for businessmen and bad for young women. For the businessman, rich, red rubies are a sign that a gamble that was recently taken will turn out well. But for a young woman to dream that she loses one is to be warned that her lover's present ardour will soon turn to indifference.

Sand is not a good omen. Just as little of any worth grows in the sands, so little of any worth will grow in the dreamer's life.

Sapphires should bring a gleam to the dreamer's eye for they presage that good fortune is about to beam down on him. And if the dreamer is a woman, she will choose well in deciding which of her numerous suitors to marry.

Silver may be something we prize in life, but as a dream symbol it is not something to be treasured. It warns that the dreamer has come to depend too much on money and because of this, happiness and contentment will never be achieved. If silver coins cascade through your dreams they suggest that you are too quick to jump to conclusions, especially in pointing out shortcomings in others.

Stones and pebbles warn that the way ahead is a perplexing one with numerous failures in your path, causing you to trip up again and again. Small pebbles indicate that the problems that lie ahead will be little more than irritations. Throwing a stone at someone means that you will have to use your authority and call a colleague or friend to order. Walking along a pebble-strewn path tells a young woman that she may be tempted by the charms of rivals for her affections.

Sulphur acts as a warning that the underhand actions of others are about to disrupt your life but that rather than confront them face to face, use discreet means to gain the upper hand. If the sulphur is burning, then the foundations of any wealth you have accumulated could be about to be shaken badly. Eating sulphur is not something that titillates the taste buds, but to dream that one is doing so indicates a hale and hearty constitution.

Tar warns that someone treacherous will stop at nothing to make the way ahead as bumpy as he (and it usually is a he) possibly can. And if the tar in question is seen on the dreamer's hands, then imminent grief and sickness will be hard to avoid.

A-Z OF DREAMS

● ●

Topaz says those who dream of it will enjoy deep friendships and good companionship throughout their lives. But for a woman to dream that she loses something made of topaz warns her to be on the lookout lest recently made friends prove to have wormed their way into the dreamer's circle for their dubious purposes. To be given something made of topaz, on the other hand, suggests that she is about to embark on a brief love affair that will go unnoticed and that will end amicably on both sides.

Turquoise, when it makes its occasional appearance in dreams, tells the dreamer that in achieving an ambition of some sort, he or she will bask in the approval of family and friends.

A Bestiary of Dreams

Animals, from antelopes to zebra, appear regularly in our dreams, be they chasing us, attacking us or simply as part of the dream landscape. Wild animals prowling through our dreams add colour and excitement and danger. Domesticated animals usually appear in calm, placid dreams. That said, a happy, playful dog can, in one rapid movement of the eye, turn into a snarling wild dingo scavenging the outback, and the cat that we are gently stroking one moment may acquire stripes and fangs and be transformed into a terrifying tiger the next. The significance of the bestiary of the creatures that inhabit our dreams is explained in the following pages. Freud, as perhaps has come to be expected, put a sexual connotation on dreams featuring animals. Other interpreters generalized, believing that to dream of domestic animals foretold happiness while wild animals were symbolic of enemies. Generalizations aside, individual animals, tame or wild, large or small, have often been designated their own meanings.

Alligators and their cousins, **crocodiles**, have few natural enemies in the wild, but are the enemies of

many creatures who cohabit their territories. Dreams
of being attacked by one of these lethally toothed
aquatic creatures, suggest that the dreamer is
insecure in many aspects of life and is especially
concerned that enemies are plotting against him.

Antelopes indicate that if you really strive, achieving
your highest ambitions is more than likely. Sadly,
though, if a young woman sees an antelope slip, then
the love she hopes to win will prove her downfall.

Apes swinging through the dream landscape bring
humiliation or illness to a dear one. If the ape is clinging
to a tree then beware, for you have a false friend who
is about to cause ill-feeling in your family or extended
family circle.

Bears rearing up in your dreams mean that you will
overwhelm any competition. Killing a bear foretells that
those entangled in intricate affairs will be able to extricate
themselves successfully if that is what they really want.

Boars, curiously, don the mantle of weather-forecaster
if they root through dreams, as they are indicative of
stormy weather brewing. In a non-meteorological role
they predict storms of a different nature being blown in
by the actions of an evil-minded enemy.

Buffalo stampeding through the prairies of your sleeping mind indicate that obstinate enemies are plotting against you. But diplomacy should see you victorious over them. A woman who dreams that she kills a buffalo, is about to embark on a significant enterprise that, successfully completed, will bring her praise from male colleagues.

Camels ambling across the dream landscape acknowledge the dreamer's awareness that he is being asked to bear more than his fair share of life's burdens, but that he will put up with the situation patiently until others agree to take some of the load.

Cats, worshipped by the Ancient Egyptians as gods, feared by those who believe in such things as a witch's link to the Devil, bring different messages as they pad elegantly through our dreams. To be scratched by a cat is an unlucky portent, to be nuzzled by one suggests that treachery and deceit are on the cards. To kill one suggests that the dreamer will triumph over his enemies. If the dream cat is black, then beware. Unlike its living counterpart, which is a symbol of good luck to the awake in many parts of the world, such a cat suggests that evil in some shape or form is about to take shape. Kittens on the other hand are symbolic of joy and peace and harmony in the home. But if the little cat unsheathes its claws and scratches you, then marital harmony will be hard to find.

Cattle, a symbol of wealth in many parts of the world, bring the same meaning to the dreamer. On its own, a cow symbolizes Mother Earth and may indicate that the dreamer has a yet-unacknowledged desire to return to a simpler life than is at present being lived. A bull seen in dreams is usually taken as an erotic symbol and many interpreters suggest that its appearance means that a male dreamer is aware subconsciously that in matters of personal sexuality, all is not as it seems. A bull bellowing in a woman's dream may be the subconscious telling the dreamer that her sex-life could be improved.

Chameleons charm those who watch them with their ability to change their colour to match the background. In dreams, sadly, they point to the fact that someone is being cheated mercilessly by an acquaintance. And *that* someone is the dreamer.

Dogs are one of the most popularly dreamed of dream animals. It's the way the dog behaves rather than the individual breed that is significant. That said, bulldogs suggest that the dreamer is blessed with a wide circle of loyal friends. To dream of hounds, be they fox, stag or any other type, warns the dreamer that schemes being laid will end with no profit being made. If the dog, any dog, is friendly, then the dreamer can depend on friends to help out in times of need. If it is snappy on the other hand, betrayal may be about to be experienced. And to be bitten by a dog is symbolic of suffering from an injury at the hands of a friend.

Deer running through a dream, according to gypsy folklore, presage that disputes with one's sweetheart are in the offing. And if the deer in question is a fawn, then the quarrel will be about the other's inconsistency. To dream of killing a deer makes it likely that you will receive an inheritance from an old man – if the deer in question is a hart, likelihood turns to certainty – and that the deceit of an unknown enemy is about to be exposed. If the hart is running fleet-footed through the dream, then wealth is about to be offered, but it will be achieved through subtle rather than obvious means.

Dolphins, long seen as friends on hand to sailors in distress, tell the dreamer that he or she may be about to be plunged into unexpected adventures. But if the dolphin is seen floundering out of water, then it could be that a sweetheart or a friend is about to disappear from the picture.

A-Z OF DREAMS

Donkeys and their cousins, **asses** and **mules**, are known for their patient endurance. It is appropriate then that to dream of them suggests that patience is the virtue required for overcoming an obstacle standing in the dreamer's path. If the beasts are behaving badly, snapping and biting, then the dreamer should beware a member of their household behaving in an underhand manner.

Elephants are a good omen. To see yourself surveying the world from a howdah, atop an elephant's back, indicates that significant, solid wealth will trundle your way and that honours, which you will wear with suitable dignity, will be bestowed on you. Business colleagues and family alike will accept whatever you say with the utmost respect. If a herd of those wondrous beasts fills your dreams, then the wealth coming your way will be very significant. If you dream that you are feeding an elephant, your efforts to help the community in which you live will be recognized and suitably rewarded.

Ferrets are well known to country folk for their sly, wicked nature and this is reflected in their place in the vocabulary of dreams as signalling that sly acquaintances are using underhand methods to work against you.

Foxes are wily creatures and if you see yourself chasing one in your dreams, then deep in your heart you are well aware that any speculations you are engaged in are dubious to say the least, and any love affairs risky in the extreme. If a fox is seen sneaking into a dream garden, the dreamer should be warned that envious and sly friends are undermining your reputation. Killing a fox, though, presages success in any undertaking to which the dreamer wishes to turn his or her attention.

Frogs springing through a dream suggest that good fortune will spring up in many aspects of the dreamer's life. But if the frog's appearance is accompanied by a feeling of revulsion then there is something in the dreamer's life that is making him unhappy and now is the time to seek out what it is.

Kangaroos bouncing through a dream mean that the dreamer has a cunning enemy who is plotting to bring about some sort of public disgrace. But take heart! Victory belongs to the dreamer. An attacking joey foretells that the dreamer's reputation is threatened: if the dreamer attacks one of these marauding marsupials, then the dreamer will overcome enemies and any obstacles that need to be cleared.

A-Z OF DREAMS

Leopards, those most elegant of big cats, forewarn that misplaced confidence may endanger plans that seem set for success. But if the dreamer slays the beast, victory is his or hers in any dispute. A leopard padding to and fro in a cage, says that the dreamer is surrounded by enemies but that they will be seen off.

Lions king of all they survey, empower the dreamer with a driving force that will take him or her by surprise. Surviving an attack by a lion heralds victory in any conflict: being defeated by one forewarns that an enemy's attack will be sucessful. A lion baring its teeth threatens those seeking more power, especially in their careers, with defeat. But a dream filled with a lion's roar tells a male dreamer that he will find favour with the opposite sex.

Lynx warn that calculating enemies are determined to thwart business matters and cause disharmony in the home. For a woman to dream of a lynx, she should take this as a warning that she has a rival in affairs of the heart. If she kills the dream lynx, she will see off the living rival.

Monkeys warn that fawning friends will flatter to get their own way at the dreamer's expense. A young woman who dreams of feeding a monkey will be betrayed by such flattering. But if the monkey is dead, then enemies will cease to feature in your life.

Orangutan bellow unfaithfulness of some sort. Perhaps an acquaintance is using you to further his own ends at whatever cost to your friendship. For a young woman, to dream of this primate portends an unfaithful lover.

Oxen symbolize sacrifice, strength and patience. In dreams they can indicate a desire to be cast in a subservient role. Two oxen indicate that good times are just around the corner, especially if they are yoked to the plough. Scraggy beasts, though, indicate lean times in the offing.

Panthers distress a dreamer and denote bad influences working against him or her that may result in contracts being cancelled or at least delayed. But if the panther is successfully slain, success is about to smile and banish any clouds looming on the horizon. If a panther's roar causes panic in the dreamer, bad news, especially about expected profits or bonuses, is in the offing.

Polar bears suggest that those who appear to be warm friends are cold-hearted deceivers.

A-Z OF DREAMS

● ●

Rhinoceros. If a rhino roars into your dreams, its presence foretells that a loss of some kind is looming on the horizon. The trouble it foretells is often of a secret nature – something you do not want the world and his wife to know about. If, however, you dream that you kill a rhinoceros (despite the fact that it is a protected species) you will leap courageously over any hurdles in your lane.

Seals suggest that the dreamer is aiming too high in his ambitions and will struggle to fulfil his goals.

Shellfish and **molluscs** may be grouped together for the purposes of dream interpretation. For although they have various meanings, they often feature together in the rockpool of the dreamer's mind. **Clams** advise that thriftiness will pay off, even if some plans have to be temporarily shelved. **Crabs** have been cast in the role of bearer of news that a lawsuit may be looming, which if lost, could be financially ruinous.

Tigers may be a threatened species but if you see one prowling towards you, you will be threatened by torment and persecution by your enemies. And if it pounces, you will fail in some venture and be shrouded in gloom. But if you see off the attack, success will bless all your undertakings.

A BESTIARY OF DREAMS

• •

Zebras, according to gypsy folklore, indicate
misplaced friendship and ingratitude. But other
dream analysts hold that these fleet-footed creatures
suggest that the dreamer will enjoy successful if
fleeting enterprises.

A Body of Dreams

Dreams concerning the human body, its function and malfunctions are among the most common, which is hardly surprising when it is probably the thing with which dreamers are most familiar.

Abdomens suggest that the dreamer has put himself in a vulnerable position, probably in a recent business venture or in a shift in responsibilities in the workplace. To dream of a large abdomen is indicative of the dreamer's hopes of good times ahead, while to see a small stomach is indicative that the dreamer fears that the road ahead is not going to be particularly smooth.

Abdominal pains are said, in converse manner, to tell dreamers not just that they are in a reasonably good state of health but that their lungs are strong and their legs especially shapely! But if the pains are in the lower abdomen then the horizon could become clouded by family problems.

Abscesses presage good health particularly if the dreamer sees himself as undergoing an operation to have one removed.

A-Z OF DREAMS

Ankles, if dreamed as being sprained, warn the dreamer to expect to experience pain in the upper region of the body, particularly the head, face or shoulders. If the ankle is broken then it's time to prepare yourself for your crowning glory to lose its lustre and begin to turn grey.

The anus when seen in a dream suggests that the dreamer stands accused by those close to him or her of being childish or behaving in an unacceptably egotistical fashion. If the anus is excreting then the dreamer is being told that in matters of the heart it is time to let go of the old and look to the new.

Arms wrap themselves around the dreamer in a variety of ways, each of which has its own meaning. For a man to dream that his arms have become bigger and stronger means the male members of his family will help him to achieve his dreams of wealth. The same dream experienced by a woman, tells her that her husband will grow in rank and status. Strong arms generally are a good sign. Generally they indicate good fortune. More particularly, if the dreamer is unwell, then he is well on the way to recovery, and if the dreamer is in prison he will soon be free. Broken arms in a male dream signify loss of authority in career matters or that a male relative will suffer ill health. If the dreamer is a woman, the same dream warns that her husband may fall seriously ill and worse, he may not recover. Death of a male relative or friend is also presaged by a dream of an arm having being cut off. If the dreamer sees the arm being amputated then death is also forewarned: a male friend or relative if it is the right arm, female if it is the left.

Backache warns a female dreamer that unless she wraps up when she ventures out, even for a moment, in bad weather, then she will be stricken with illness.

Backbones do not feature very often in dreams, but when they do they are a good omen, presaging a healthy, happy life made even happier by being the centre of a loving family.

Baldness is not a warning that the dreamer's hair is about to fall out. Rather it tells him or her to keep calm no matter what difficulties present themselves in the future. A bald person who dreams that his crowning glory has miraculously grown back can expect to be lucky in love, or if he already is, then exceptional marital harmony is on the horizon.

● ●

Beards often sprout in dreams. To see a beard getting longer and bushier signifies a boost to the bank balance. A non-bearded man who sees himself sporting a wispy growth on his chin should take it as a warning that he may be about to become involved in a lawsuit. To dream of having a beard trimmed risks a great loss of property or worse that he is running the risk of dying in a most unusual and unexpected way. To see one's beard being washed says that sadness lies in store. To dream that it is being pulled out by the roots is worse – great danger is lurking.

Blindness suggests that you have put your trust in someone who will prove to be a false friend. If the dreamer owns a business of any sort, then he or she may well be let down by trusted employees. It also warns the dreamer to be extra attentive to his or her partner in life because he or she may be about to stray from the marital bed. Losing one's sight can also be a warning that affluence is about to fly out of the window leaving the rest of one's life to be lived in abject poverty. If the dream concerns someone else's blindness, then someone the dreamer holds in some esteem will unexpectedly ask for assistance.

● ●

Blood seeping into dreams is not something to be welcomed. Friends will prove to be false and a sweetheart will look elsewhere for affection. Those involved in the business world who have pinned their hopes on a big deal coming off should think again. It won't!

Bones seen sticking out of the body are a sign that treachery is about to strike. If the bones are piled up like Tamerlane's Tower then let's just hope the larder and medicine cupboard are well stocked, for famine and ill health are about to feature in the dreamer's life.

Brains say that the dreamer is unhappy and becoming increasingly irritated with his or her surroundings. It could be the house or home, or it could be that it's friends and acquaintances who are crowding in on the dreamer, making him feel swamped and desperate to be given his own space.

Breasts can herald good news and bad! If the dreamer sees her breasts as plump and full, then good fortune will soon be hers. If saggy and wrinkled, rivals in affairs of the heart will outdo her and steal her lover's affections. If either breast is wounded in any way, then a mild bout of ill health is suggested.

A-Z OF DREAMS

Breathlessness is a bad sign, especially if you are involved in a scheme that seems to be on the verge of success. Hiccups will interrupt things and just when you least expect it, success will be snatched away at the last minute to be replaced by insurmountable failure.

Constipation says to the dreamer that it is time to let go of the past in all aspects of life, and that if behaviour patterns are changed the dreamer will reap significant benefits, especially emotionally.

Ears warn you to listen out for rumours that someone you know and trust is playing a waiting game, watching your every move until there is a hiccup in business matters or squabble in the home. He or she will then do everything to make sure that the blame is heaped on you and in doing so show themselves in a better light.

Elbows that are dreamed of covered in scabs, foretell of minor annoyances that will grow to major disturbances in business life, and that sadness lies in wait.

Eyebrows presage that the immediate future is blocked with a sinister obstacle of some sort.

• •

Eyes are not to be welcomed, warning as they do, that enemies are on the lookout for the slightest chance to make mischief, either in business affairs or in matters of the heart. If it's the former, then whoever is plotting will use extremely devious ways to achieve his ends. If it's the latter, then a rival is just biding his time before trying to worm his way into a sweetheart's regard. And in both cases, if the dreamer is not careful, the loss will be theirs. If the colour of the dream eyes is striking, then the colour itself is more significant than the eye. Brown eyes warn that deceit is all around. Blue eyes suggest that while the dreamer has good intentions, the will-power to see them to fruition is probably lacking. Grey eyes suggest that their owner is open to flattery.

Feet are an unwelcome symbol to the dreamer. To dream of one's own feet is to be warned that you will be forced to submit to the ill-tempered will of another and that this will cause huge despair. A dream of washing your feet is indicative of the fact that you are letting others walk all over you, while to dream that your feet are sore warns that you will come off worse in a family dispute and that your defeat will be humiliating. If they are red and swollen, then family scandal will cause you to be separated from your family and this will cause a sudden change in business fortunes. The only good news about seeing feet in a dream is when they belong to another. Then, they tell that you will get your own way if you are determined to do so without having to resort to unpleasantness, and that in doing so, your reputation will be enhanced.

Fingers and **thumbs** have their own meanings as well as being an integral part of the hand (also see Hands). The first finger points the way to being more expansive in all aspects of life, while the second one says that some sort of restrictions lie ahead. The third finger warns that the dreamer is far too preoccupied with him or herself. And the little finger suggests that matters concerning communication will come to the fore. The thumb tells that the dreamer is well aware of the power that he holds over others and that he is determined to wield it wisely. If it is seen pointing upwards, then renewed energy and vigour will soon stride towards the dreamer. If it is pointing downwards, life is about to take a turn for the worse. It certainly did for Roman gladiators whose performances in the ring failed to please spectators!

● ●

Fits warn that a bout of ill health is about to lay the dreamer low and that this could cost them their job. To see someone else have a fit suggests that employees or juniors in the work place will cause some sort of unpleasantness.

Foreheads that are line free and smooth denote that the dreamer has a reputation for fairness and good judgement. Lined, worried foreheads suggest that your most private affairs are about to cause you a great deal of displeasure.

Hair has about as many meanings as there are hairs on the human head! For a woman to dream that she is combing a head of thick, lustrous hair warns her that she will neglect her personal affairs and that in doing so her career will suffer. Men who dream that they are going bald or that their hair is thinning are being warned that their generosity will cost them dear and that some sort of psychological illness might be threatening. A woman who dreams that she is losing her hair tells her that she will have to work hard to earn her living. Hair that is turning grey presages a death in the family or in the circle of closest friends. Snowy white hair, on the other hand, presages a life full of

● ●

fortune. Hair that is dreamed of by men as turning pure white overnight while the face stays young and unlined warns of extremely bad news coming soon. For a woman to have such a dream is a warning that a sudden illness or accident will rob her of her lover. For a man to dream that he has thick, black curly hair tells that although he is seen as hugely charming by women, they don't trust him. And for a woman to dream that she has similar hair suggests that someone she trusts implicitly might be about to try to seduce her. Male dreamers who see a woman with shining gold hair are being told that women see them as true friends and fearless lovers. Red hair in general suggests change is on the horizon. And for a man to dream that his lover has red hair tells him that she is being or will be unfaithful. Brown hair is bad news for dreamers who are considering a first career or a change of job: the choice they make is likely to be the wrong one.

Hands, the parts of our bodies that we all use, often unknowingly, when we express ourselves, express themselves significantly in the sign language that is dreams. If they are seen holding different objects, then some sort of conflict is presaged, probably between what the dreamer believes in and what he feels. If a hand is seen clamped across the breast, then the dreamer is about to submit in a situation that has long been bothersome. If the hands are clasped, a new friendship is indicated or perhaps an existing one is about to deepen into something special. A hand clenched into a fist warns the dreamer of a looming threat. If the hands are folded, then the dreamer is being told that it is time to relax and rest more. Hands covering the eyes suggest that the dreamer has done something about which he is deeply ashamed or even horrified. Someone who feels that restrictions of some sort are in place may well dream of a pair of hands crossed at the wrists. If a hand is offered to another person, then the dreamer is acknowledging that surrender may be the only way to unblock the path ahead. If the palms of the hands are facing outwards, then the dreamer is being told to give the blessing for which he has been asked. But if the hands are pressing on either side of the head, then the dreamer is being advised to think long and hard before taking the course of action to which he is being pressed. Washing your hands in a dream is a sign that the dreamer considers himself innocent of some charge that has been levied against him.

Headaches warn that worry will pile up and start to weigh the dreamer down. If a young woman dreams that she has a headache, she may be worried that in

● ●

seeing off a rival in the game of love she has put herself at risk of being at the centre of vituperative gossip.

Heads have various dream meanings. If it's the dreamer's head that's seen then nervous problems could be about to strike. If the head is of the severed variety, then dreadful disappointments lie in store and reasonable hopes are about to be dashed. If the dreamer sees two heads growing from the shoulders, rapid career advances are in the offing, followed by just as rapid demotion. A child's head means financial success is just around the corner.

Heels may help take the weight of our bodies, but as Achilles found out after they were the only part of his body not washed with the waters of invincibility, they can be the weakest part. Certainly, in dreams they suggest that the dreamer is feeling vulnerable about something and that the worry is growing deeper and deeper.

Ill health can herald good news or bad news for the dreamer. A woman who dreams that she is incurably ill can look forward to being healthy and well looked after for the rest of her life. But to dream of being mildly ill is a warning to take care, not just in health matters but in life in general. (Also see specific complaints.)

●●●●●●●●●●●●●●●●●●●●●●●●●●●●●●●●●●●

Jaws talk of disagreement, especially disagreements among friends, especially if they (the jaws that is) are ugly and malformed. If the jaws are normally formed but they are aching and painful, then a move to a different climate is on the cards, and a bout of illness may well cause a financial loss of some kind.

Kidneys are a vital part of the body's cleansing system and when seen in a dream they say that now is the time to flush out problems.

Knees, if dreamed of as being too large, are a sign that ill health is about to strike. If they are painful or stiff, something significantly dreadful is waiting to knock you for six! If the dreamer is a woman and she dreams of having smooth, shapely knees then although she may, indeed will, have many admirers, none of them will walk her down the aisle.

Limbs in general suggest that the dreamer is having doubts about his or her sexuality. If an arm or a leg is being pulled from the torso, then these doubts are literally tearing them apart, and threatening them to the very roots of their existence. If sexuality is not the issue, and arms and legs are seen again and again then we are being told to dismantle our lives and start again.

A-Z OF DREAMS

Lips, that are full and luscious and red, say to the dreamer that good times are just around the corner – if they have not already shown themselves. Relationships will hum harmoniously and there are affluent times ahead. If the dreamer is in love, then lips such as these indicate that the love will be reciprocated. Swollen lips, on the other hand, speak of sour marital relations, ill-tempered meetings and being forced to make decisions that will turn out to be the wrong ones. Thin lips whisper to the dreamer that he will be able to master the details of any subject to which he turns his mind.

Lungs may warn that the clouds of grief are forming on the horizon and are about to blow in to darken the dreamer's life. Alternatively, they may flag the fact that very important decisions can be put off no longer and have to be made right away.

Muscles, if they are as well developed as an athlete's, signify that enemies are about to show their unwelcome faces but that you will see them off and come out of the experience with increased wealth. If the muscles are underdeveloped, then if you think you see success beckoning, relax: it's calling someone else.

Necks, if they belong to the dreamer, warn that there are family members, maybe members of the extended

• •

family, who have a grievance about some business matter, perhaps a will, and that in airing it, your business affairs will be adversely affected. If it is someone else's neck that features then the dreamer should beware that someone close, very close, sees them as being too worldly for their own good. And if a woman dreams that her neck is too swanlike, she should learn to control her temper or else she will become so increasingly shrewish that her children will bring forward plans to leave the nest. Worse, her husband may flee with them!

Nudity often features in dreams. If dreamers see themselves in the nude, then scandal is in the wind and if the dream occurs just after appointments have been made, it may be best to consider cancelling them as they could have unexpected and unwelcome consequences. If the dreamer sees himself being suddenly discovered in the nude and desperately tries to conceal himself, then he is feeling guilty about something – usually some illicit pleasure that has been very much enjoyed. If other people are dreamed of in their naked state, then temptation will be put in your path. If a young woman sees herself admiring her naked form in a mirror, then she will win the respect and regard of an honest man – but not for long.

A-Z OF DREAMS

•••••••••••••••••••••••••••••••••••••

Pain, if it is the dreamer's, suggests that some trivial action will lead to regrets that are out of all proportion. If it is someone else's pain, then the dreamer is being warned that too many stumbles are being made in the march along life's path. If the discomfort is more of an ache than a pain, then the dreamer is not being bold enough in business. He or she may have some very good ideas but in not promoting them strongly enough, others are profiting.

Perspiration suggests that the road ahead is blocked with some sort of difficulty that will see you as the centre of unpleasant gossip. But don't get into a sweat about this. The difficulty will be overcome, the gossip will turn to words of praise and you will emerge from the experience with your honour intact, indeed enhanced.

Rheumatism warns that plans being laid will be plagued with unexpected delays, if it is the dreamer who is affected. If it is someone else in the dream who is stricken, then disappointments will crop up when least expected.

Ribs that are obviously healthy signify wealth, but if they are in poor condition then poverty will loom large in the dreamer's life. If the upper ribs are broken, and the dreamer is a man, then he is about to have some sort of disagreement with his wife and she will emerge victorious. If the lower ribs are broken, then the argument will be with female relatives rather than the wife, and that once again the distaff side will win! If dreamers of either sex see their ribs growing larger and stronger it means a happy marriage is on the cards.

Scratching the head tells you that fawning strangers are annoying you with their unctuous flattering, which, you are well aware, is self-seeking ingratiation of the most blatant kind.

Shaving tells male dreamers that they are masters in their own household and that even though wives and daughters may occasionally rebel, they will not do so for long. If after shaving, the face is seen as smooth, this reinforces the message of a dream shave. But if it is aged and lined, then marital storms are about to blow in. If a man dreams of being shaved, he is being warned to be on the lookout for impostors who are out to defraud him. A woman who dreams that her face is being shaved is showing her concern that she is being too masculine, especially in career matters. If she dreams that she sees a man shaving, then she will be overindulged by men and she will be the worse for it.

A-Z OF DREAMS

• •

Shoulders dreamed of as naked say that the dreamer will shrug off any bad luck and that changes of a pleasant nature will make him view the world in a much nicer way.

Skeletons when seen in dreams warn of oncoming illness or, worse, injury inflicted by someone who has misunderstood something you did or said and is out for revenge. If the dreamer sees himself as a skeleton, then he is worrying unnecessarily about something and should lighten up. If a skeleton is seen as haunting the dreamer, then there is trouble ahead – serious trouble: a fatal accident or financial disaster.

Skulls signify that there are domestic squalls about to blow in, which, while they will die out, will leave an atmosphere of suspicion that will linger for some time. If it is the skull of someone known to the dreamer, then a friend is about to turn enemy because the dreamer has in some way been preferred. If it's the dreamer's own skull that is seen, then he or she is about to rue something said or done.

Sneezes signify a change of plans is on the cards, if the sneeze is your own. If it is someone else's sneeze then you are about to have unexpected visitors who will bore you to distraction.

● ●

Tattoos needling themselves into your dreams are an unwelcome sign that something is about to happen that will necessitate a long and extremely boring absence from home. If the tattoos are decorating another's body, then someone is jealous of you and their jealousy is eating away at them, which may lead them to take unpleasant action.

Teeth have almost as many meanings as there are teeth in the human jaw! To see ordinary teeth in a dream suggests that illness is about to strike or that new acquaintances may turn out to be wolves in sheep's clothing. Loose teeth warn that bad news about a business failure is probably already winging its way towards you. If a tooth is being extracted, then a serious bout of ill health is waiting in the wings: the only good news is that it will not turn out to be fatal, although it may be touch and go! Dreams of losing one's teeth warn that pride goes before a fall, especially in business matters. To have a tooth knocked out means bad luck will come out of the blue. It could be a business failure or it could be the death of a loved one. This litany of bad luck gets worse if the teeth are yellow and crooked for such teeth herald loss of property, a bout of bad health (probably affecting the nervous system) and being let down by a business partner. If one tooth falls out, then look for bad news in the morning's mail. If two come loose and fall out the circumstances over which the dreamer has no control will cause unhappiness. For three to fall out, a serious accident is presaged. And if the dreamer sees himself as having a full set one minute and being toothless the next, then hunger is about to gnaw at the dreamer's innards. The only time teeth smile on the dreamer is when dreamers see themselves gazing in a mirror admiring their mouthful of white, even teeth, for then their plans for future success will be brought to happy fruition.

Tongues, if they belong to the dreamer, are unwelcome in the dream landscape for they tell that for some reason friends will frown on the dreamer and that unless the dreamer mends his or her ways, then friendships may well start to evaporate. If it is the tongue or tongues of others that feature in dreams, then the dreamer is being warned that he may well find himself at the centre of some scandal. To dream of a swollen tongue or one that is otherwise in poor condition tells the dreamer, literally to watch his tongue! If the warning is unheeded, careless talk could well cost lives!

Wombs suggest that the dreamer is seeking security and shelter and that he feels he has been asked to shoulder an unfair share of responsibility and that now is the time that the burden be removed.

A Wardrobe of Dreams

The clothes that we wear in our dreams are believed by some interpreters to show the side of ourselves that we want the rest of the world to see. Others see them, when they are the dominant theme of a dream as indicative of a deep-seated desire not to be touched by other people. In covering up our naked state, dream clothes conceal the imperfections that we believe we have and perhaps our true sexuality. And the parts that they cover, or reveal, may indicate ways in which we believe ourselves to be vulnerable. If the colour of the cloth is the thing that the dreamer recalls most strongly, that is probably more significant than the articles of clothing themselves. And if a dreamer sees him or herself wearing the clothes of the opposite sex, then he or she is being told to be more aware of their feminine and masculine sides respectively. This is especially true for women who dream that they are wearing a male uniform of some kind.

Applying make-up denotes success in life. If the dreamer is in love, it indicates that her sweetheart is faithful, good-humoured and keen to tie the knot as quickly as possible. If the dreamer is already

• •

married, then any children you have will be very
successful. To see someone else putting their make-
up on is to be warned that false friends have
unpleasant surprises in store.

Aprons tell a female dreamer that the plans she has
laid for the future will go helter-skelter but to stick with
them, for they will come to fruition – eventually. And if
the dreamer is still at school and she dreams that she
is wearing a loose apron, or one that is torn, she is
being warned that her nose may be about to be
forced to the grindstone, for her inattention has been
noted by her teachers and her parents.

Bags are generally a good thing to see in your
dreams. If you are carrying one that is full, you might
not acquire great wealth, but you will never go short. If
it is so full that you can hardly carry it, let alone shut it,
then significant wealth will be yours. But if the bag is
hanging loosely from its strap and is obviously empty,
then poverty may well afflict you.

Bonnets and **hats**, new and seen by female
dreamers, according to some act as a warning that a
love of finery, a desire for admiration and the envy of
friends could land them in hot water. According to
others, new bonnets mean new love – and his

behaviour will be determined by the colour. If it's green, he will be deceitful, blue and his affection will be long lasting, as opposed to pink which suggest that he is something of a fly by night, and if it's yellow or white he will propose marriage with almost indecent haste. If a woman dreams that she loses her hat then she may find that her reputation is the subject of some discussion among her friends. If the wind takes it, then she should be on the lookout for sticky fingers for something she prizes could be in danger of being stolen. And if an unmarried man dreams of a girl's hat his bachelor days are numbered for a determined woman has set her cap at him!

Bracelets are thought to herald marriage to a wealthy person, but not necessarily a happy marriage.

Brooches' dream meanings depend on where you see yourself wearing them. If you're at home, then a friend may be about to put a business opportunity your way – and it could be a winner. But if you are wearing one in the company of strangers then you could be in danger of being robbed.

Buckles bring bad news to female dreamers if they see themselves as having lost one, for doing so means that an important agreement she has made or has been made on her behalf will be broken and she will be all the worse off for it. Buckles also say that invitations are about to flood in and that in trying to cope with them all, chaos could reign – especially in business affairs.

Changing clothes suggest that the dreamer has a desire to change his or her image and that now is the time to do it.

Cloaks, according to gypsy folklore, suggest that the dreamer will go to any lengths to conceal things that worry him or her, particularly regarding financial matters, from friends and acquaintances.

Clothes, in general, if they are dirty tell the dreamer that strangers met in the immediate future may appear to be friendly, but they should not be taken at face value. If the dreamer is a woman and the clothes she is wearing are dirty and torn, then new friends may damage her good reputation. If her clothes are in pristine condition, then prosperous times lie ahead. And to dream that you are spoilt for choice indicates to older dreamers that they may have trouble in providing for their families in the not too distant future. The same dream experienced by a younger person says that ambitions and hopes may be about to crash on the cliffs of disappointment.

● ●

Coats say that the dreamer needs to be protected from something, either physical or emotional. And if there is a fear that the coat be lost, then the dreamer is thought to be concerned that faith or beliefs that have been long held may be about to be challenged and the dreamer is uncertain as to whether he can withstand the pressure. If the coat is not long enough to cover our legs or not thick enough to offer warmth, then we may have fears that the protection we built up – financial, spiritual or emotional – may not be adequate to cover our needs when the time comes. If the coat is torn, your last years are going to be marked by unhappiness. Your children will move far away and if you need financial support it's no use looking to them for it – they will ignore your appeals. But if you dream that you tear the sleeve of your coat then that's a sign that if you were thinking of starting a new business then now is the time to do it for if you work hard at it, success will follow. And to dream that the coat you are wearing is beautifully tailored and fits perfectly is a warning that financial problems are coming up fast on the outside rails and are about to overtake you. If you dream that you have lost your coat then don't be tempted to speculate in the immediate future: to do so could cost you dear.

A-Z OF DREAMS

● ●

Colour is important, especially if it is that rather than the article of clothing itself that is recalled by the dreamer. To see yourself dressed in white is a sign of guaranteed success in the next project you undertake. To dream that you are wearing green heralds a journey that will end in you hearing something very much to your advantage. Black clothes, with their associations with funerals, are generally believed to suggest that bad luck is nearby. Blue clothes denote happiness and red or scarlet warn that some sort of sadness might be about to make itself known. To be wearing yellow can be good or it can be bad: but opinion seems to be that it is a lucky colour to be dressed in – just! Crimson clothes denote a long and healthy life. And if, like Joseph, you dream that your dream coat is one of many colours, then life will be one of ups and downs – good times and bad times – and that, for most of us, is life!

Corsets warn the female dreamer to keep her counsel, for given the slightest provocation she will pick a quarrel with friends and as a result the friendships may come to an end, or at best cool a little. They can also suggest that the wearer is the centre of a new admirer's attentions that she finds unwelcome.

134

A WARDROBE OF DREAMS

● ●

Crinolines, no longer as common as they once were, but still used for some bridal gowns, suggest that money will be short and the woman who dreams of one will be forced to cut her cloth accordingly.

Dirty clothes have long been seen as a warning that shame of some sort is about to disgrace the dreamer.

Dressing in a dream suggests that you have recently done something of which you are not too proud and would rather keep to yourself.

Embroidered clothes signify that the road ahead is one lined with happiness and honour.

Fur coats, once so desired, but now seen as cruel to the animals that unwillingly donate their pelts, warn the dreamer not to enter into serious arguments for the immediate future. If the warning is ignored, the argument will degrade into a quarrel that could lead to a serious family split. On the brighter side, furs can indicate that things are going to go well in the immediate future, especially if the dreamer is involved in buying or selling a property. And for a young woman to dream that she is swathed in fine fur is a sign that she will marry not a particularly rich man, but a very wise one.

A-Z OF DREAMS

● ●

Gloves have as many meanings as they have fingers!
They can represent the need to cover and protect
oneself, or they can indicate that the dreamer has had
enough of a particular situation and is willing to 'take
the gloves off' and challenge the way things stand at
present. To dream of putting on a glove and keeping it
on is an indication that marriage is in the air. And so
does a dream of having difficulty in trying to squeeze
a hand into a glove that is too small, in which case
dreamers of either sex can expect to receive a
proposal at any day. To receive a pair of gloves in a
dream suggests that you will have rival lovers and
find it almost impossible to make your mind up
between them.

Hair shirts suggest that the dreamer has done
something in the past that he or she now deeply
regrets and feels the need to do some sort of
penitence for it.

Handkerchiefs (cloth ones as opposed to paper
tissues) suggest that the dreamer is a flirt and enjoys
wearing his heart on his sleeve. If one is dreamed of as
being lost, and the dreamer is engaged to be married,
then the engagement will be broken off through no
fault of anyone. A torn handkerchief warns that lovers'
tiffs will become more frequent and deepen to such an

extent that the relationship will break down never to be mended. Yucky, used ones say that the dreamer should be more careful in their choice of friends, if they want to avoid being corrupted in some way. Pristine, white ones on the other hand indicate that silver-tongued flatterers are whispering in your ear. Ignore what they say and you will marry well: listen to them at your peril! Coloured handkerchiefs tell that morality is not the first word that comes to mind when the dreamer is being talked about, but such is their charm that no one seems to mind.

Hats (also see **Bonnets**) are thought to be symbolic of wisdom and, as they shelter us from the elements, they are believed to be concerned with our need to feel protected when they feature in our dreams.

Lacing up shoes is believed by many to be symbolic of death – not necessarily a physical death but perhaps a farewell to someone the dreamer has known for a long time and whose friendship and wisdom he values.

Linen clothes are comfortable to wear and good to dream of, unless soiled. Fresh, clean linen says that good news is about to come your way, and that your

● ●

current love is the one you will spend the rest of your life with in complete harmony. But if the linen is grubby, poverty may be about to rear its unwelcome head, love might be about to evaporate from a relationship and if that wasn't enough, then something you treasure could go missing.

Negligees herald adventure in the love department, especially if the dreamer comes into contact with another who confesses to a similar dream! If the negligee is still in its box or bag, friendships being forged now will be long lasting and the source of a great deal of pleasure. And for a man to dream of a woman clad in such a garment is a warning that he will be strongly tempted to stray from the marital bed, and that if he yields to it, the consequences will be almost unbelievably far reaching.

Nightgowns tell the dreamer that career prospects are excellent, unless he sees the gown being taken off either by himself or another. In this case the dreamer is afraid that the consequences of some hasty and ill-considered action are about to bear fruit – and it will be too bitter to swallow! They can also warn that the dreamer may be about to be laid low for a few days with a cold or some other mild affliction. To see others in their nightgowns warns that there may be a downturn in business or career matters, and sad news about a friend not seen for a while may be about to be heard. If a love struck young man sees his girlfriend in her nightdress, then it's more than likely that another will take her place in his affections.

Overalls and suspicion for some reason walk hand in hand across the dream landscape! For an unmarried woman to dream that her boyfriend is wearing overalls serves as a warning that he is not all he has cracked himself up to be. And for a married woman to see her husband overall-clad is to be given advance notice that next time he claims to be away on a business trip, the business may not be the one in which he works!

Perfume when received as a gift in a dream heralds good news if it is a scent that the dreamer likes. If it is not to her or his tastes then the news will be as disagreeable as the perfume. Good news is also predicted if the dreamer sees him or herself giving someone a bottle of scent and it obviously pleases the recipient.

Pyjamas, with the connotations of bed and relaxation, indicate that the dreamer would like to be more open about certain aspects of his life – sexuality perhaps – but is unsure how to go about it.

A-Z OF DREAMS

● ●

Raincoats are yet another symbol of the need for protection, this time from an onslaught on the emotions. They can also indicate that the dreamer would like to return to the womb, in the short term at any rate.

Shirts can be good or bad – it depends on the state they are in! If they are torn then it could be that someone is spreading slander about the dreamer. If the rent is self-inflicted then it is the dreamer himself who has been indiscreet about someone and is worried that the consequences will be dire. But if the shirt is in pristine condition, then success in a recently embarked upon venture is certain. To dream of putting on a shirt suggests that the dreamer will enjoy a trouble-free spell for the time being and that travel to a foreign country is on the cards. There is a proviso to the last meaning: if the dreamer has recently embarked on a new affair, it's not going to last long, for he will soon be tempted to lay his head on another's pillow. Shirts can also mean that no matter what life throws at you, you will boy-scout-like smile and whistle through all your difficulties. To dream of losing a shirt is a sign that business is going to go through a bad patch or that love affairs are heading for trouble.

● ●

Shoes tell us that we have our feet on the ground and that we have our finger on the pulse. But if the shoes are curiously designed then the dreamer may be being warned that he needs to take a fresh look at his attitude to life in general and that if this is done, the benefit will be felt in many departments of the dreamer's life. There is an old superstition that it is unlucky to put shoes, especially new shoes, on a table. This has spilled over into the dream world where such shoes are thought to be symbolic of death, physical maybe or perhaps in the form of a farewell to an old acquaintance. To dream of wearing new shoes is to be told that travel is in the air. And, curiously, to dream that one is shoeless suggests a comfortable and honourable life. If the dreamer sees shoes falling from the feet it indicates poverty and distress. And if the shoes are scruffy and down at heel, then you will be short of cash more often than not.

Silk dresses have two quite contradictory meanings according to two dream experts from days gone by. According to one, for a woman to see herself dressed in silk is a sign that, if unmarried, she will soon meet her lover who will be rich, and if already wed, her husband will become wealthy. But the other interpretation suggests that for a married woman to see herself dressed in silk is a sign that her husband is being unfaithful with a woman who will cause him financial distress.

Squeezing into dream clothes that are obviously too tight suggests that the dreamer has outgrown things that were once a source of pleasure and is looking around for new amusements.

Stockings or **tights** warn to be alert for trouble or distress of some sort, for it is not far away. And if they are laddered or have holes in them then best mend your ways if you don't want to be the subject of wagging tongues. If the stockings are white, a mild bout of illness may be ahead. Stockings can also mean that the dreamer is about to look for his or her pleasure in places associated with the dissolute and among people who most regard as unsavoury.

Taffeta dresses tell the women who dream they are wearing them that they will be wealthy, but that money doesn't buy happiness!

Ties are seen as representative of a desire for correctness and discipline in the dreamer's own life and business and in those of his friends and colleagues.

Umbrellas offer us protection from the elements and are, appropriately enough, seen as symbols of protection in dreams. To see yourself sheltering under one is a sign that you have done well in laying down plans to protect you and your family from hardship. If you tear or break the brolly, you may find yourself having to shoulder the blame for something you didn't do or that just when you need the support of family or friends, they let you down. To receive an umbrella as a gift is a signal to keep your ears open for some good advice from a friend or colleague. And to dream that you lose one is, curiously, a sign that you are about to receive an unexpected gift.

Underclothes cover our most intimate parts and accordingly are thought, when dreamed of, to be concerned with our most intimate secrets.

Underskirts suggest that the dreamer is regarded by her friends as something of a social butterfly and one who puts far too much importance on her possessions. If the petticoat is dirty, there's a danger that the dreamer's reputation is being blackened. If an unmarried woman dreams that she is wearing a new petticoat, it is a signal that she will marry a man regarded by many as 'a man's man' but that he will dote on her. A petticoat seen falling off when the wearer is at a party suggests that the dreamer is in for a disappointment of some kind, more than likely in her romantic life.

Undressing is a warning that the dreamer is the subject of unjust gossip and try as she will to stop it, the tongues will go on wagging for quite a while.

Uniforms suggest that the dreamer has influential colleagues and friends keen to help him climb the ladder of success. If uniforms feature in the dreams of a young woman then the man on whom she bestows her affections will return it – in spades. But if she sees herself slipping out of a uniform and changing into more relaxing attire, her love of adventure will lend a note of notoriety to her name to such an extent that she will find herself at the centre of a scandal of her own making! Dream characters wearing strange uniforms suggest that disruption is in the air – a friendship that has run its course and is brought to an end, perhaps.

Veils either covering someone else's face or your own suggest that whoever is wearing them has hidden agendas and may resort to dishonesty before showing their true hand. If matters of the heart are on the dreamer's mind, then deep down he is well aware that he has not been totally sincere with his lovers and when this is revealed, underhand methods may have to be used to retain their affections. If a young woman sees herself losing her veil then her lover realizes that she may have been unfaithful and what's sauce for the goose... Bridal veils herald welcome change in the dreamer's life and for a young woman to dream that she is wearing one is a suggestion that a recent investment has been a wise one and will pay handsome dividends. But if the veil comes loose, there's sadness in the air.

Velvet clothes appropriately signify that honour and riches could be there for the asking, if the dreamer recognizes the opportunities that come his or her way and grabs them.

Wardrobes have two meanings, both of which depend on how full they are. Seen bursting with clothes it suggests that in trying to appear better off than the dreamer really is, he is putting what money he already has at risk. If the wardrobe is almost empty, then flirtation is in the air: not of a romantic nature, but flirtation with danger. Beware!

A Rainbow of Dreams

Colours, according to tradition, highlight certain aspects of our life. If they are clear and bright, they indicate positive aspects and trends either existing or on the horizon. Conversely, dull colours have negative associations for the dreamer. And, as one would expect, each colour has its own significance for the dreamer.

Black, traditionally associated with death, does not tell dreamers that their days are numbered. Rather, it signifies that a phase in the dreamers' lives is coming to an end. A job maybe, a relationship, or, to parents, that they fear the day that looms when children will flee the nest and leave home, leaving a gap that the dreamer dreads. It also indicates passive acceptance of the situation.

Blue offers the dreamer protection from pressing problems and says that the future can be faced with renewed confidence and restored hope. It does have a negative side (what doesn't in the lexicon of dreams?). If the dreamer takes too calculating and cold a view of life then depression may set in.

● ●

Brown, not the most popular colour in the waking world, is not the most inspiring in the dreaming one. Dull devotion to duty is called for. But if that's a depressing thought, cheer up. For the quicker duty is done then the sooner the dreamer can turn his or her attention to the brighter things in life.

Gold, the colour of sunshine, has a very simple message for the dreamer when it floods into his or her dreams. Happiness lies ahead, and the brighter the gold, the longer-lasting and more fulfilling the happiness will be.

Green is thought to be the most relaxing of colours (hence its widespread use in hospitals and schools in the not too distant past). When it dominates a dream, it is telling the dreamer to relax, take time out and have a few early nights. But it can also indicate that the dreamer is allowing envy and jealousy to influence decisions both in matters of the heart and the home.

Indigo is the colour of instinct and intuition. It tells the dreamer that there is more to life than the physical and that just as the body needs feeding and exercising regularly if it is to function properly, the soul and spiritual side of things need nourishment and stimulation.

• •

Orange has two or three distinct meanings when it paints the dream landscape with its warm, cheerful hues. It can mean that the dreamer is subconsciously scrutinising social relationships and is willing to consign those that are unrewarding or unsatisfactory in some way to the out tray in his social life. It can also mean that a dull life is about to be brightened in some unexpected way. And lastly it can mean that trivial matters are about to surround the dreamer. Each one on its own comparatively insignificant, but taken as a whole, then time-consuming and tedious to cope with.

Red is the colour associated with strength and physical energy. It can mean that renewed vigour is about to flow through the dreamer's veins, making him ready to face any challenge that life may throw in his face! It can also be taken as a warning that rage and anger, if allowed to go uncontrolled, will have an adverse affect.

Violet, like indigo, tells the dreamer to fuel the altruistic and spiritual side of things and that if this is done, then the benefits will spill into every aspect of life.

White, with its associations with purity and honesty, predicts that innocent pleasures and freedom from pressures lie ahead. But it can also indicate that the dreamer is subconsciously aware that his life is colourless.

Yellow, the colour associated with cowardice, suggests that the dreamer is afraid of facing a confrontation that he is aware is looming but will put off dealing with until it is literally staring him in the face. But the colour suggests that if positive thinking is used and that the dreamer lets his head rule his heart then all will be well.

A Family of Dreams

The family and other people are among the most common images seen in dreams. We may see ourselves doing a variety of activities with people we recognize – shopping with a spouse or climbing a tree with a sibling. And often it is the activity that is more important than the other person. But it may be the other person's significance that is important, or their behaviour or attitude or their manner. A dream of an argument with a member of the family, for example, can only be interpreted if we know the dreamer's relationship with the family member argued with in the dream – father, mother, cousin or whatever and how they interact with the dreamer in real life. To dream of being a member of a harmonious family signifies health and an easy life, but if there is sickness and argument, then gloom and disappointment is presaged. But little is that simple, for family figures can represent themselves or they can stand for that part of the dreamer that has foundations in that particular family member ...

Adolescents, if of the opposite sex, suggest that the dreamer is suppressing a part of his or her

development. If the dreamer sees himself as he was
as an adolescent then he may be acknowledging that
some part of himself has still to mature. Often dreams
of adolescence say that the dreamer wants more
freedom to act as he wants and that he or she resents
the freedom which others seem to enjoy.

Ancestors often crop up in dreams at times in our
lives when we are asking questions about who we are
and why we are here.

Aunts, when they are seen smiling, say that any slight
differences that have been clouding the atmosphere
will soon be blown away to be replaced by pleasant
surprises. If the dreamer is a young woman, though,
the appearance of an aunt in a dream suggests that
she (the dreamer) is about to be upset by being
censured for some action of which she considers
herself innocent.

Babies tell us that we have to recognize that we
have feelings deep inside us over which we have
absolutely no control and probably never will have.
Very often babies feature in our dreams when we are
planning a new venture. If the baby is someone else's
rather than one's own then the dreamer is being
reminded that other people have the ability to hurt and

● ●

should always be treated with respect. If the baby is a particularly bonny one, new opportunities could be about to present themselves and if grasped, they could be exploited to the dreamer's advantage. If it is crying and obviously not well, then the opportunities could well lead to increased responsibilities. Dreaming of giving a baby away suggests that the dreamer feels overburdened with responsibility and wants to lighten his or her load.

Boyfriends tell the female dreamer that they still have not found their life partner yet: especially if it is a former boyfriend. If the boyfriend is someone the dreamer has never seen in that role before then she is being told that she needs to reconsider the way she relates to men.

Boys, when seen in dreams, remind dreamers that they have the potential for growth no matter how old they are – it's never too late.

Brothers, in dreams as in life, can be friend or foe! Seen active and full of energy, they say to the dreamer that good fortune is about to smile if not on the dreamer, then on someone close. If, on the other hand, the dream brother appears to be poverty stricken and asking the dreamer for help of some sort,

● ●

then good fortune is about to turn her back on you, to be replaced by loss of a glum kind. More generally, dreaming about a brother is often a sign that the dreamer is becoming increasingly aware that there is some sort of uneasiness within the family and that the way to resolve it is to bring it out into the open.

Children seen in dreams remind us that there are parts of us that are and probably always will be childish. When we recognize this we are well on the way to becoming more rounded people so when children feature in our dreams, it may well be the subconscious's way of telling the dreamer that the time for that recognition has come. They are generally regarded as being a positive image, especially if they are in obvious good health and playing happily. It is hardly surprising that children, not necessarily the dreamer's own offspring, feature often in the dreams of parents when you think of how large they feature in adults' lives, their capacity to cause problems, their capacity to surprise and their capacity to bring unparalleled joy into life. If it is one's own offspring seen in a dream it is thought to be a good sign, suggesting that the immediate future will be especially cheerful. For a mother to dream that she has many beautiful children is a sign that many blessings will be brought to her by her offspring. If the dream concerns a child who has had a little accident, she will be upset by lots of little niggles – nothing serious, but annoying all the same. If the child is hard at work at his or her books, then a period of prosperous calm is heralded. To dream of a child stricken by illness suggests that its welfare (not necessarily its health) is under threat. And although dreams of a dead child may be extremely upsetting, they don't forewarn the child's death, but rather that worrying or disappointing news is in the offing. If the child is seen as being disappointed in some way, perhaps crying or frowning then acquaintances who appear to be friendly are, in fact, being duplicitous.

Congregations herald bad news. At best some sort of unpleasantness will affect the dreamer, and should be taken as a warning to the dreamer to be very careful when dealing with friends, or else he may find himself alone when he most needs to depend on the kindness of friends. At worst such a crowd of people can suggest that the unpleasantness will be very unpleasant indeed – it could mean that death will affect the dreamer: maybe not his own, but of someone close!

Cousins, the relations that most of us see at occasional family events – weddings, christenings and funerals – just as occasionally pop up in our dreams. When they do, sadly, they presage that the way ahead is fraught with disappointment and perhaps physical affliction of some sort. If the dream concerns writing to a cousin, then relations between the two branches of the family could be about to take a downward turn. On the other hand, dreaming of receiving a letter from a cousin says that you may be about to hear that an old love is keen to rekindle the flames of passion. Good news or bad news? That depends!

Crowds suggest that the dreamer is unwilling to be singled out for any one attribute and would prefer to stay in the background, out of the limelight in most aspects of life. That may be all right for some, but it could suggest an irresponsible attitude to life. If the crowd is well dressed and perhaps enjoying some sort of entertainment, pleasant times lie ahead in the company of convivial friends. But if anything happens to mar the crowd's enjoyment, then friendship may be about to desert the dreamer's life to be replaced by unhappiness. The change in mood can also indicate dissent in the family. If the crowd is in a street then the dreamer's business will perk up and prosperity beckons. If the dreamer is shouting to make himself heard above the noise of a crowd, then he may find himself standing accused of pushing his own interests above those of others. According to Jung, an outwardly calm person who dreamed of a crowd was, deep down, in a state of some agitation!

Daughters, when seen in a dream, suggest that there are stormy times blowing in but that, as with the weather, nothing lasts for ever, and the storm-force winds will die down to be replaced by calm and pleasant times.

Daughters-in-law often have uncomfortable relationships with their husbands' mothers, and when they feature in a dream they signify that some unusual event is about to occur. Good or bad? That depends directly on how the offspring's wife is behaving. If she's smiling and happy then something unusually nice is heralded. If she is scowling and glum then something unusually nasty might be round the corner.

Dictators - be they well known tyrants such as Hitler or Stalin, or an autocratic and overbearing boss perhaps – feature in the dreams of those who have been brought up by extremely strict parents. When they are dreamed, such dictators may be saying the dreamer is still concerned that he or she is still not living up to the standards that the parents set, or that the child has disappointed the parents in some other way.

A-Z OF DREAMS

● ●

Dwarfs augur that the dreamer's health is sound and that he will be very unlucky if he is prevented from achieving his dreams because of ill health. The same meaning is given to dreaming that one's friends have magically shrunk!

Fathers traditionally underline that parent's love for their dreaming child and are a sign that they will always be there for their children. But they have other meanings, too. Sometimes, to dream of your father suggests that a difficulty of some sort lies ahead and that you will need some very good advice (perhaps from a legal expert) if you are to extricate yourself from it. If the dead father appears in a dream, it could be that there are business difficulties ahead and you may have to put the brakes on a deal you were keen to go ahead with. If the dreamer is a young woman and she dreams that her father is dead, she should keep an eye on her boyfriend or husband because, to use a sporting term, he may be playing away from home!

Fathers-in-law warn that there is contention in the air, unless particularly jovial, in which case the family relations are going to be very harmonious.

● ●

Giants suggest that we are starting to come to terms with some of the feelings concerning adults that we repressed as children. They may have scared us in some way but the subconscious is telling us that if we get rid of these feelings our emotional lives will be all the stronger for it. They can also represent anger that we have been repressing. And if we can get rid of it, we will be better able to cope with problems that arise – especially emotional ones. On another level, the appearance of a giant in our dreams can indicate an upturn in business and general prosperity. But nothing is that simple in the language of dreams, for giants are also said to herald a struggle of some sort. If the giant stops you from moving on, then enemies will get the better of you, but if he backs off then good health and prosperity are yours for the taking.

Girls tell male dreamers that it is time to get in touch with the more innocent, sensitive side of their characters. If the girl is one who is known to the dreamer then he is already aware that these qualities exist in him and that if he occasionally tried to look at life from a female perspective then life may be all the better for it. If the girl is unknown then it is time to acknowledge that they exist and take it from there.

A-Z OF DREAMS

Grandchildren are a sign that the dreamer is hankering after his or her own childhood and that this is evidencing itself in talking about 'the good old days' far too much for the family's liking.

Guardians, perhaps more Victorian than twenty-first century, rarely feature in dreams. When they did (and if they now do) they told the dreamer that friends were going to be especially considerate. If the dreamer was a girl and her guardian was scowling at her, the frown indicated that there was trouble in store, probably a financial loss of some sort.

Guests, unexpected and seen arriving in large numbers, say that it may be time to say 'Goodbye!' to old friends because friendship has run its course, sadly!

Gypsies travelling through a sleeper's dreams suggest that there is a wanderlust about to stir in the dreamer and that he or she will go to some lengths to satisfy it. The wanderlust may be physical, or it may be that the dreamer wants more freedom to conduct his life as he thinks fit. To dream of a gypsy encampment says that you will receive what looks like a good offer of some sort but that when you look into the background of the people who make it, you will have second thoughts – and rightly so! If a woman dreams of having her fortune told by a gypsy, she is in danger of rushing into a marriage that she will come to regret. If she is already married, her husband may be about to start accusing her of showing quite unwarranted jealousy.

Hermits are normally regarded as symbols of sorrow when they make their lonely presence felt in a dream. The sorrow may well be brought about by the unthinking actions of friends.

Husbands leaving home in dreams, warn a woman that choppy waters lie ahead on the home front but that they won't last long and marital harmony will soon be restored. If he is being unkind, then relax, for he holds you in high regard and will continue to do so throughout the marriage. If, however, he is seen to die, then there's disappointment in some form or other ahead. If your husband appears pale and burdened with cares, then someone in the family may be in for a long bout of ill health that will see you run off your feet trying to cope.

Kings say that you are over-ambitious but that you will have to work hard to make your dreams come true, unless you are being crowned in which case you will be promoted above the heads of your fellow-workers. And if you are being told off by a king, then you will stand accused of neglecting your duty. But to dream of talking to a king is indicative of a rise in reputation. And if His Majesty gives the dreamer something, then some sort of gain will follow. If the dreamer is a woman and she sees herself in the company of a king, then, according to gypsies, she will come to fear the man she marries.

Men, if they are tall, dark and handsome tell the dreamer that enjoyable times are round the corner, and that if they are already here, then they will get even better. But if the dream male is not blessed in the looks department then for good times read disappointment! If the dreamer is female, a male in a dream signifies that she should look to her masculine side and if she does this she will increase her chances of success in business. If her dream man is indeed a dream man, then she will find herself being offered a distinction of some sort, maybe in her career or maybe as recognition of charity work. If, on the other hand, he is ugly, someone she thinks of as a friend will bring her trouble in some shape or form. An older man is thought to represent the innate wisdom that lies deep within us all.

Mothers are the first people with whom dreamers forge their first significant relationships. So it is not surprising that they feature so often in dreams. If your mother appears in your dream as she is in real life, then she is giving her blessing to any enterprises you are involved with and they should turn out well. If you are talking to her, then you will soon receive good news about a business that has been concerning you. For a woman to dream of her mother tells her that her marriage will be happy and that her life will be full of pleasant duties. If the dreamer sees his or her mother as emaciated or worse, dead, then huge sadness will follow, while to hear her cry out as if in pain is almost as bad – for there is menace in the air. To hear her call out warns that business colleagues think you have been making bad decisions or that you have been derelict in carrying out your duties. And being such important figures in our lives – there is more about mothers. If a man sees his mother being transformed into another woman he is being told that it's time to let his mother go: that other women are just as important, if not now then perhaps later.

Mothers-in-law say that there's going to be a serious disagreement some time soon but that peaceful relations will soon be restored and the reconciliation will find the relationship, be it a family one or a friendship, is strengthened as a result.

A-Z OF DREAMS

Nephews smiling through a pleasant dream say that good news, perhaps concerning a windfall, is about to be received. If, on the other hand, the man is frowning or is seen as being uglier than he is in real life, then there's some sort of disappointment ahead: nothing serious, but a disappointment just the same.

Nieces, when seen in the dreams of a woman, warn that the immediate future will be peppered with worry caused by totally unexpected events.

Orphans, if they are unknown to the dreamer, warn that other people's unhappiness will affect the dreamer in some unexpected way, making him or her change the plans he or she was laying for some sort of pleasure. If a relation is dreamed of as being orphaned, then more and more duties will be piled on your shoulders and these will create a gulf between you and some of your friends. Dreams of orphans can also predict that a complete stranger is about to benefit the dreamer in a totally unexpected way.

Pirates are indicative of the fact that there is something in the dreamer's personality that is subjugating the emotional side. To dream of them is often seen as a sign that the dreamer feels that he or she is losing control of some aspect of life or, for a woman, that she feels that her partner has too much say in the way she behaves. To dream that you are a pirate is to be warned that you will fall from grace and former friends and family will come to look down on you. If a young woman dreams that her lover is a buccaneer it portends that he is unworthy of her love and will deceive her cruelly. If she is taken prisoner by a pirate, the silver-tongued words of someone will persuade her to leave home and that if she does she will soon realize she has made the wrong decision. For a male dreamer to be taken prisoner by a pirate suggests that he feels under threat of losing control of some aspect of his life.

Queens signify that the dreamer will be successful in anything he or she cares to turn their hand to, unless the monarch is old and haggard in which case pleasures will recede to be replaced by serious disappointment.

Sons, if they are dreamed of as being unusually good looking, can be regarded as a sign that the boy will be particularly successful at anything he puts his mind to and will bring great honour to the family. But if he is in any way blemished or seen suffering from illness or the results of an accident then there is trouble in store.

A-Z OF DREAMS

Sons-in-law, curiously, do not feature in the dream dictionary!

Stepsisters are not a thing that too many people have and therefore do not pop up very often in dreams. If you have one, and if she does appear in your dreams then you are about to be put upon, not necessarily by her, and will be unable to avoid the annoyance and inconvenience that this will cause.

Uncles may be good fun in real life, but when they make an appearance in a dream they warn that news of some sort that will cause a family dispute is on the way.

Widowhood is not a happy state for most women and when a woman sees herself as one, she is being warned that malicious tongues are wagging and that their gossip will cause her much distress. If a man dreams that he is getting married to a widow, then his best-laid plans, probably business ones, are about to go totally awry.

Wives, no matter how happy the marriage in real life, tell the dreamer that the immediate future may be a bit unsettled, unless they are unusually jolly, in which case recently made investments will pay off handsomely.

A FAMILY OF DREAMS

● ●

Women have several dream meanings one of which is that intrigue could be being plotted behind the dreamer's back. If the dreamer is arguing with a woman then the plotters will be foiled. To see a dark-haired woman suggests that for some reason you will drop out of a race in which you were thought to have had a good chance of success. If she has auburn hair a period of anxiety could soon hit the dreamer. And if she is a blonde, then the anxiety gives way to pleasure.

A Menu of Dreams

Food and eating feature in many dreams. Some of the symbolism is obvious – dreams of famine presage bad times ahead, dreams of banquets can foretell good times. But sometimes, as so often in dreams, the meanings are not so plain to see.

Baking may be less and less common today, living as we do in a shop-bought world. But it does still waft its way into the dream kitchen and when it does beware. To a woman it means ill-health and being burdened by having to look after too many children – not necessarily her own. To a man who is already in a position of having to look after others, the demands on his pocket will grow even more of a strain. Baking bread in the company of others is a good sign, predicting that as the dreamer makes his way through life, the more competent and assured he will become.

Banquets suggest that any favour you ask of a friend will be granted. But if you are eating alone then no matter how fine the fare, misunderstandings will lead to acute disappointment. If the banquet is in full swing when you arrive, then you are about to be caught up in matters that will upset you in some way.

Beef is an unwelcome intruder into the dreamer's world unless it is being properly served with some ceremony. If it is, then harmony in love and business is suggested. If the meat is being badly carved, then misfortune beckons. Raw beef signifies serious ill health. Cooked beef is even worse: the loss of a loved one may be about to devastate the dreamer's life.

Beer warns that plots are being brewed against you by what you had assumed to be convivial friends.

Brandy promises wealth and distinction in the dreamer's chosen career, but that those whose good opinion they aspire to will detect a certain coarseness which will prevent them from extending the true hand of friendship to the dreamer.

Bread being eaten brings few crumbs of comfort to a woman dreamer. Her children may be charming and pliable youngsters but the older they get the more stubborn they will become and the more worry and fruitless work they will cause her. To see stale bread warns that the dreamer will be burdened down with unhappiness. Crusts warn the dreamer to look to his duties, for if he is careless and incompetent in performing them, then misery in some form will loom large.

Breakfasts can be good or bad. Eating them in the company of others is a sign that you are on an even keel, but if you are breakfasting alone then you have enemies who are laying a trap of some sort for you.

Butter when dreamed of being eaten signifies good health and that plans well laid will come to successful fruition. But if the butter tastes rancid, then the most the dreamer can expect to achieve in his life is a reputation for competency.

Cabbages presage that a lover is wearing his or her heart on the sleeve. If those in wedlock have not yet strayed from the marital bed, then they are certainly considering doing so, while those whispering words of love to an unmarried partner are simply repeating what they are also saying to another. If the dreamer is cutting the heads off cabbages then he is being told that profligate expenditure will prove to be ruinous.

Cakes are good to eat and with one exception good to dream about. They tell the dreamers that they have given their hearts to the right person and that they will inherit a house in which they will be very, very happy.

They predict that hard work will bring its just rewards in time and that friendly society will always be close at hand. But for a woman to see a wedding cake is not a happy omen, suggesting as it does that her life will be one of hollowness and superficial friendships.

Carrots tell a young woman that she will marry young and that she will give birth to a string of bonny babies that will live long, healthy lives. To other dreamers, carrots indicate that prosperity and health can be taken for granted.

Celery suggests that dreams of prosperity will not only be achieved, they will be far surpassed. Eating it alone says that love will warm you for as long as you live. For a girl to dream of eating it with her lover signifies that she will inherit considerable wealth.

Cheese of any sort except, according to one authority, Swiss cheese, is not a welcome sight to the dreamer, signifying as it does sorrow and disappointment about to influence life. If the dreamer is able to recognize that the cheese of his dreams is Emmenthal or any other Swiss variety, then that lone voice claims that it is a portent of a large inheritance.

Chickens and other poultry warn the dreamer to mend his or her ways or else extravagance will cause increasing hardship. If a young woman dreams that she is chasing poultry around a farmyard, her life will be one of frivolous pleasure and she will come to be seen as the shallow creature she is.

Chocolate presages that the dreamer will have more people than he planned for looking his way for a step up in life. But the good news is that he will find the means to provide for anyone who looks to him for assistance, which will be gladly given.

Cocoa has the reputation for appearing in the dreams of people who make friends with those who they think will help them to advance professionally and socially rather than those who they really like. And worse, the friends cultivated are usually distasteful to others of the dreamer's acquaintance.

Custard tells a married woman to prepare for unexpected guests, and a young woman that she will encounter a stranger with whom she will forge a lifelong friendship with no romantic strings attached. If the custard has been oversweetened, then an event being looked forward to with pleasure will turn out to be tinged with sadness or regret.

A-Z OF DREAMS

Dinners dreamed of eaten alone are a sign that now is the time to turn your thoughts to making sure that future needs are well catered for.

Drinking chocolate warns that there are business reverses approaching but that the dreamer will see them off and prosper even more than before.

Drunkenness can be a good thing or a bad thing: it depends on what the dreamer has been drinking! If spirits are the cause of inebriation beware, for your reputation for overindulgence may well be about to cost you your job. Having drunk too much wine, on the other hand, is good news, especially for those with literary ambitions, for this dream presages success in that direction.

Eating in good company is a sign that your plans will prosper and the friends you have will be true. But if you are eating alone, loss may be about to hit you and melancholy wrap you in its wings.

Eggs when found by the dreamer in the nest, suggest that wealth will soon be his. They also indicate marital bliss for couples who have already taken the plunge and that the union will be a particularly fruitful one. But if the dreamer is eating eggs, then domestic affairs are about to be influenced by something totally unexpected and very unusual. To dream of broken eggs is a sign that fortune is about to rain down on you. But if the dreamer sees himself being pelted with eggs, then any wealth that comes his way will be of a very dubious nature. If the eggs dreamed of turn out to be rotten, then property is about to be lost or something of a particularly degrading nature is about to happen. A tray of eggs should encourage the dreamer to join a speculative venture that has recently offered itself, for it will turn out well.

Famine, as we said earlier, warns that there are bad times just around the corner: that seeds scattered in business will not germinate and flourish: that sickness may be about to afflict the dreamer. But, if you see business competitors suffering famine, then their misfortune proves to be your good luck.

Flour and frugality go hand in hand in the kitchen of dreams. But frugality does not necessarily indicate unhappiness. Indeed for a woman to see herself dusting flour from her hands means that she will be happy to subordinate herself to her husband but that in return he will make sure she has a pleasant life.

A-Z OF DREAMS

●●●●●●●●●●●●●●●●●●●●●●●●●●●●●●●●●●●●●

Garlic, when seen growing, gives you a flavour of the success that will come your way regardless of how humble your origins. And although for a woman to dream of this pungent bulb promises happy marriage, it will be one entered into from a sense of duty rather than for reasons of love: that will grow with time. Eating garlic denotes that the dreamer is of a sensible nature and that with his feet planted firmly on the ground, he is happy to leave matters of an idealistic nature to others.

Ham in general warns the dreamer that there is treachery in the air. But if the dreamer is carving a ham in generous slices, then all opposition will be sent packing. If it is being eaten then something of value is about to go missing.

Honey spreads happiness and wealth in the dream lexicon, with one exception. To dream that you see honey foretells that wealth will wing its way to you. To dream of eating honey augurs well for those looking for love and those who are already smitten will find that their love grows so quickly that marriage plans will be brought forward. And the exception? If a young woman dreams that she is making honey from the comb, then disharmony will rear its unwelcome head in domestic matters.

● ●

Horseradish gives advance notice to a woman that she can expect to move up the social scale and that in her new position she will find herself mixing with interesting, clever people.

Hunger signifies that disharmony is about to hit the home of those who are married, while those who are planning their wedding who dream that they are hungry may as well call the whole thing off, for marital happiness will never be theirs with their current love. If the hunger is acute, then something that you had thought of as being a huge success is about to end in failure.

Ice cream being eaten by the dreamer suggests that business affairs will soon be licked into shape. If children are enjoying it, then fortune will smile on those whom the dreamer holds dearest. If a young woman dreams that she spills it or that some dribbles onto her clothes, then she will gain a reputation of being a flirt – and it will be quite justified unless she mends her ways.

Jam is a good omen in the language of dreams as it augurs nice surprises, especially ones concerning travel. And for a woman to dream that she is making jam tells her that she will be the centre of a happy home and a wide circle of extremely nice friends.

● ●

Macaroni seen in large quantities tells the dreamer that if strict economies are made in any direction, the dividend will far outweigh the sacrifice made. But to dream of eating it, warns that losses may hit the dreamer's pocket – not large, but a loss is a loss! If the dreamer is a young woman and she sees uncooked macaroni, then she can expect a stranger to enter her life and influence it in an unexpected way.

Marmalade is said to have been given its name by the chef to Mary, Queen of Scots while she was married to the dauphin of France. When the young princess fell ill, the young chef concocted a jelly of quinces and herbs for 'Marie malade' and the two words became corrupted to the one we know today. Maybe that is why to dream of marmalade warns that a bout of ill health is on the cards.

Meals in general suggest that the dreamer is paying too much attention to too much detail in business matters and that this is stopping him seeing the overall picture.

Meat, if cooked, and dreamed of by a woman, warns her that what she is working towards will be snatched from her and given to another. If the meat is

• •

uncooked, then she will achieve her goal, but only after she has overcome discouragement from many directions. For dreamers of either sex, roast meat is a sign that a spouse, if not already being unfaithful, may be on the verge of being so. If the dreamer is carving a joint of meat, then an investment recently made will have been ill-judged. But it's not too late to withdraw and look elsewhere.

Milk has a variety of meanings for the dreamer. Farmers can expect a good harvest and travellers safe passage. To dream that one is giving milk away warns that overgenerosity may cause problems in financial matters. Spilt milk warns that the actions of a friend will cause you short-lived unhappiness brought about by a loss of some kind. To dream of milk that has gone off is prescient of lots of niggling problems coming up – nothing serious but distracting nonetheless. Reaching for a glass of milk that stays Tantalus-style, just out of reach, signifies that a valued friendship is about to come to an end abruptly or that something of value will be lost. To dream of hot milk promises that ambitions will be realized but only after some hard-fought battles have had to be won. And lastly, to dream of bathing Cleopatra-like in milk indicates that the companionship of good friends will soon warm your life.

● ●

Omelettes, when being eaten warn that somebody regarded as an equal by the dreamer is about to impose upon him, probably financially. And flattery and deceit are likely to be experienced by the dreamer if he sees himself being served one.

Onions being sliced and bringing tears to the eyes, suggest that you will soon feel the sting of defeat at the hands of a rival. But otherwise, dreams in which onions feature herald good things. They tell of success (although the more there are, then the more will be the amount of spite and envy your success will generate). Dreaming of eating them presages that you will see off all opposition in your way to the top. If the onions are seen growing, then the rivalry you experience will make life interesting and you will learn from it.

Overeating, when dreamed of by a woman, warns her to mend her ways if she is to escape the sharp comments of others.

Parsley being eaten portends good health. You may well need it for it could mean that you and your spouse have a large family. To see it growing suggests that success will come but that it will be hard won.

Parsnips are good for the businessman, not so good for those looking for love. To the investor they suggest that resurgent trading conditions will boost financial markets. But to the lovelorn they say that there is little chance of finding true love in the immediate future.

Picnics are usually enjoyable affairs and this enjoyment is mirrored in their meaning to the dreamer – success and a cloud-free sky are just ahead. If the dreamer is young, then hugely enjoyable times lie in store. But, if the elements interfere and the picnic is abandoned, then there may be hiccups in love and business affairs.

Potatoes, unless they are dreamed of rotting, promise plenty. To dream of planting them, portends that long-held desires are about to be realized. To see oneself digging them up promises that success will soon be harvested. If the potatoes are being eaten, a significant gain of some sort is about to be made. And to cook them suggests that career matters are bubbling along nicely and will get even better. The downside to potatoes sprouting in dreams is that if they are mouldy or rotting, then the pleasure in life will soon be a thing of the past and a dark future lies ahead.

● ◆

Punch, for some reason, is often reported to feature in the dreams of those who have a reputation for being self-centred and who enjoy their pleasure at other people's expense. So if you dream that you are enjoying the punch bowl, perhaps it is a warning that it is time to mend your ways.

Radishes presage that the kindness of friends will bring about business success. Eating them, however, suggests that one of these friends will act thoughtlessly and that in doing so there will be a little hiccup on the road to that success.

Rice, traditionally scattered at weddings to bring the happy couple good luck, also showers the dreamer with good tidings. It predicts success in business and that friendships made will be warm and long-lasting. Farmers who dream of rice can expect a bumper crop, and anyone who dreams of eating it is promised domestic harmony. A young woman who sees herself cooking rice can look forward to new duties coming her way, which will make her happier both in matters of the heart and the pocket! The only drawback to dreams of rice is if it is mixed with grains of soil, for featuring so in dreams warns that ill health is just round the corner and friends may move away.

Rum presages a wealthy future but an increasing liking for gross behaviour that will cost you the friendship of those who knew you while you were poor, or at least before you became wealthy.

Salt signals disharmony. Plans will start to unravel and arguments will blow up from nowhere, especially at home. To see yourself salting meat, implies that you may have taken out a larger mortgage than your income merits and that while you can afford the repayments at present, things may change for the worse. If a young woman sees herself eating salt, she will lose her love to a more beautiful rival.

Sardines suggest that unexpected and distressing events are about to muddy the waters, and if the dreamer is a young woman and she is laying them on the table, then she is about to attract the amorous attentions of someone who is distasteful to her.

Sausages being eaten indicate that while the dreamer's home will be a humble one, it will be one of warmth and happiness, which will act as a magnet to others. If the dreamer is making sausages, then he or she will be successful at whatever they may care to turn their hand to.

A-Z OF DREAMS

● ●

Sugar may be sweet, but it sours our dreams, suggesting as it does that in the foreseeable future the dreamer will find fault where there is none, particularly in domestic matters. And that this will be emotionally and financially draining. Eating sugar indicates that unpleasant matters will have to be dealt with, but that the outcome may be better than at first expected.

Tea has a variety of meanings. Dreamed of being brewed, it signifies that the dreamer will find himself charged with the crime of indiscretion, and rightly so. Forgiveness will be a long time coming. Drinking tea with friends, although it may seem contrary, suggests that the dreamer is feeling society is *jejune* and would rather put his free time to better use than simply socializing with others. To go to a tea caddy and find it empty, warns that gossip of a most disagreeable nature is being whispered about you. And lastly, someone who dreams that he is 'dying for a cup of tea' is about to have his peace shattered by unexpected and unwelcome guests.

Thirst warns the dreamer that what is being aspired to at present may prove unattainable unless the thirst is eventually quenched.

Treacle on the dream table signifies a pleasant invitation is about to wing its way to you and that in accepting it surprises of an extremely pleasant nature lie in store. But if the treacle is eaten, you will be crossed in affairs of the heart. If a woman dreams that treacle is trickling on to her clothes, then she will be surprised by an offer of marriage from someone she holds in contempt.

Turnips being eaten signify ill health is about to hit. If they are being pulled up, on the other hand, there is a general improvement in store as new opportunities will soon present themselves and a corresponding upturn in fortune will result. If they are seen growing in the field, then again, prospects are about to brighten.

Vegetables in general indicate that you have been deceived into believing yourself to be successful while all the time you have been sorely used by another. If the vegetables are rotten great sadness is about to engulf you. If a young woman dreams that she is slicing vegetables then she will cut off her nose to spite her face and cause her lover to leave. But that turns out to be no bad thing, for a new love will soon show his face and prove to be a faithful husband.

A-Z OF DREAMS

● ●

Vinegar is not to be welcomed. It predicts disharmony
in every aspect of life. To dream of drinking it indicates
that you will be forced to commit to something against
your better judgement and that this will cause you
tremendous worry. And to see yourself drizzling it over
your food, implies that something that is already
causing you distress is going to get even worse.

Whisky, when seen but not tasted tells the dreamer
that he or she can work as hard as possible to achieve
an ambition, but it will never be realized. If the dreamer
does down a dram then the dream will be achieved,
but only after disappointments have had to be faced
and overcome.

Wine promises that new acquaintances will become
increasingly good friends. But if a wine bottle is seen to
smash in your dreams, then love may turn to passion
and passion to excess. To dream of a wineglass
suggests that serious disappointment is about to cloud
your life and that the sky will stay dark until something
jolts you into taking action to restore the sunshine.

Working in a bakery suggests that there may be
career changes in the offing but that they should be
treated with some wariness as the road gets bumpier
with every corner turned.

A Jobful of Dreams

Tinker, tailor, soldier, spy. These and a host of other occupations have been and still are recorded in dreams. So, too, have the places in which we work and the tools that we use, which is hardly surprising as, after our home, it is at work where we spend most of our time. Indeed, in these competitive days, it is not unknown for thrusting young businessmen to spend more time in the office than they do with their families – during the week at least.

Actors may indicate that the dreamer is having doubts about how sincere someone close to him really is. Being a dream actor can also suggest that it's time to take the bull by the horns and take charge of one's own destiny.

Apprentices may not feature in dreams as often as they did when apprenticeships were more common and youngsters were willing to enter into them. But when they do they tell the dreamer that there could be a struggle ahead if he or she is to be accepted as an equal by companions.

A-Z OF DREAMS

• •

Artists, appropriately enough, are thought to be a recognition that the dreamer should pay more attention to the artistic side of his or her nature, something that is often suppressed, especially by male dreamers.

Bakers are extremely positive dream images. They tell us that we have the ability to change our lives if that's what we want to do and they indicate that whatever plans have been laid will turn out to be extremely successful. The only negative thing about them is that they may be telling us that before the benefits can be felt, we may need to hone our creative abilities.

Ballerinas point to the fact that deep down we are acknowledging a need for balance and poise to enter our lives.

Bankers are an acknowledgement that the dreamer realizes that he or she needs the help of someone in authority to iron out difficulties in matters financial and to get his or her personal resources in better order.

Beggars indicate that a change in life is likely and that caution should be your watchword when dealing

188

with strangers, for they may not be as trustworthy as they appear to be on first acquaintance.

Butchers, with their association with blood and death, were once thought to herald a particularly nasty death. But today, their dream meaning has changed – just a little. For death substitute a long illness that may or may not be fatal! If the butcher is cutting up a joint of meat, the dreamer may be subconsciously acknowledging a fear that he or she is the subject of some discussion among friends and the conclusion they come to may not be to the dreamer's advantage.

Caretakers and their modern-day equivalent, security guards, tell the dreamer that if he or she is a parent, his or her children will be unusually annoying in the near future. If you go searching for one and fail to find one, be prepared for niggling little annoyances that will upset your normally smooth routine. If you do find one, then strangers you meet may be so pleasant that they won't be strangers for long and could become good friends.

Carpenters are regarded as a threat to the dreamer's composure, but it's not something to worry about – things will soon be back to normal and equanimity restored.

A-Z OF DREAMS

Doctors are seen to carry good news in their bags when they pay a call in the sleeper's dreams. Often seen as authority figures, they can presage that the dreamer is seen to be doing well at work and has been marked out for promotion. They can, of course, suggest that the dreamer is worried about his or her health and is about to acknowledge that whatever may be the matter should be referred to a professional physician.

Engineers say that a journey, probably a long tedious one, is on the cards, but that at the end of the road there will be an exceptionally happy reunion with someone the dreamer hasn't seen for a long time.

Estate agents say that the part of us that is concerned with self-interest is winning the struggle against the more altruistic side of our nature, especially where matters of personal security are concerned.

Fishermen are seen as representing a provider of some sort, and with their association with 'the catch' may suggest that the dreamer is on the lookout to 'catch' a new job or a new partner.

Gaolers indicate that we are feeling some sort of restriction. It could be that our own emotions are holding us back from reaching true fulfilment or that the power of someone else's personality is shackling us in some way. They can also tell that the dreamer feels him or herself to be the victim of their own circumstances. Gaolers most often appear when the dreamer has been feeling particularly lonely.

Gardeners, according to gypsy folklore, symbolize good luck and say that plans being laid at the time of the dream will culminate in speedy success.

Hairdressers suggest either that the dreamer has a desire to change his image or that someone is trying to influence him in ways that he may not necessarily want. They can also signify that we are questioning the basis on which one of our closest relationships is founded.

Herdsmen, curiously, warn the rich that good fortune is about to frown on them and turn her attention to others – the others in question being poor dreamers who dream of herdsmen!

Judges making their presence felt in dreams are thought to warn that in trying to improve a situation, you may actually make things worse. They also suggest that before you come to any decision in the near future, things should be planned with more caution than usual. And it may be that people close to you do not have your best interests at heart and that you should take steps to protect yourself from them. According to Romany tradition, to dream of a judge or magistrate is an indication that the dreamer feels he is being persecuted in some way.

Lawyers are said to indicate that bad news or a loss, perhaps both, may strike. If the dreamer is about to enter into a contract or embark on a new business venture, the appearance of a man of the law should be taken as a warning to do some more homework before signing on the dotted line.

Looking for a job in a dream is quite straightforward for once. Being unable to find one is indicative that you are loyal to your present employer and have no intention of making a move. Finding one, on the other hand, suggests that you may find yourself knocking on prospective employers' doors in the very near future.

Masons suggest that you are about to carve yourself opportunities that will gain you promotion at work and a consequent rise in social status. If the masons are the sort who belong to the Masonic Order and they are wearing their aprons and regalia of office, then they serve to remind you that you have a responsibility towards others who look to you to protect them from the evils of life.

Mechanics herald a change of address and an upturn in business if the dreamer is self-employed. If he or she is employed in a business that has been struggling to survive, the appearance of a mechanic in a dream can suggest that business is about to pick up and then boom to such an extent that there may soon be more in the salary cheque within a month or two.

Millers say that no matter how bleak things may be at the moment, hang on in there, for they will soon start to brighten up and that despair will soon turn to hope. If the dreamer is a woman, her love may turn out to be less wealthy than he appears or pretends to be. If such matters are important to her, then she should look elsewhere for marital happiness: but if she doesn't care for material things he will turn out to be a loyal and loving husband.

Miners suggest that someone with malice on his mind is digging into your background trying to find something, anything that can be used to bring about your downfall.

A-Z OF DREAMS

Monks bring family quarrels in their wake, and may be news that some sort of unpleasant journey may have to be made. To dream that one is a monk suggests that a loss of some kind is imminent. If it is a female whose dreams a monk enters, she may be about to find herself the target of some particularly malicious gossip.

Nuns tell dreamers of religious bent that spiritual matters may be about to be pushed aside in favour of more material matters. If the dreamer is female, the good sister brings a warning of early widowhood or long-term separation from the man she loves.

Offices often suggest that we feel burdened by responsibility and that we would like to relinquish if not all responsibility then at least share it with others. They also feature in dreams at times when work has become less enjoyable than it once was and at such times tell the dreamer to search for ways to make it more pleasant.

Osteopaths are indicative of our need to manipulate the circumstances of our lives to ensure material comfort. They can also suggest that the dreamer is concerned about his health. To dream of an osteopath could say that an awareness is gradually growing in the dreamer's subconscious that he or she is being manipulated by another person or influences, either of which can be countered if that's what the dreamer wants.

Plumbers can reflect the dreamer's concern with his or her health, or they can suggest that the dreamer is something of an ostrich, burying his head in the sand to avoid confronting unsettling emotions.

Priests are unwelcome visitors in the dream landscape, for they bring bad tidings with them. If the priest is in the pulpit, the dreamer may be about to be struck down with illness. For a woman to dream that she is in love with a priest, suggests that her lover will deceive her: and if – Heaven forbid – she dreams that she is making love to a priest her love of laughter will not be smiled on by those closest to her. To see oneself in the confessional suggests that some sort of humiliation or sorrow is looming.

Sailors tell the dreamer to prepare to receive news from abroad. In days of yore, to dream of a sailor was to be warned that a dangerous sea voyage was imminent. On a deeper level, sailors represent freedom of spirit and freedom of movement and their appearance suggests that the dreamer is in control of his life more than most. That said, dreamers who see sailors in their dreams might need to seek the approval of someone in authority before making the most of that control.

Servants warn dreamers to watch their tempers for if they don't their anger will propel them into time-wasting worries and arguments that they can't win. To dream of sending a servant on his or her way never to return signifies that the dreamer will come to regret a recent action or decision or/and that a loss of some sort is about to be felt. To quarrel with one means that when the dream is over, someone – either an employee or a family member – will be found to have been derelict in duty and will have to be severely ticked off.

Soldiers warn that conflict of some sort may be about to march into the dreamer's life. The background to the dream may give some clue as to how the conflict will arise and how it will eventually be settled. The military can also say that deep down the dreamer realizes that there is a need to be more self-disciplined. And it can also mean that a change of employment is just around the corner.

Surgeons suggest that the dreamer is acknowledging that there is something in his life that is unwanted and should, if possible, be cut out as soon as possible.

Tailors warn the dreamer that an upcoming journey will cause some sort of disappointment. If the dreamer sees himself having an argument with his tailor, a recently laid plan will not run smoothly and may cost the dreamer dear.

Teachers, the first authority figures that most children meet outside the immediate family, may say that the dreamer is acknowledging the need for guidance to help overcome a problem which, while not pressing at the moment, could easily become so. They can also suggest that the dreamer has already been given some advice on how to cope with a pressing problem but that he is willing to consider an alternative – indeed would welcome one.

Thieves are linked with a fear of losing something – maybe something tangible or perhaps something emotional, but a loss nonetheless. They can also suggest that the dreamer is increasingly aware that precious time is being squandered on a useless activity.

A-Z OF DREAMS

Unemployment is not a particularly happy state when awake and is just as negative in dreams. It suggests the dreamer is feeling undervalued and is scared that he or she will not be equal to a task that has to be faced in the immediate future.

Vicars and other non-Catholic men of the cloth can herald that a period of calm is on the horizon and that any disputes will soon be settled to the mutual satisfaction of everyone involved. They can also indicate that the dreamer acknowledges that there is still much to learn, especially about the spiritual side of life. Vicars can also portend that jealousy and envy will lead you to do some extremely foolish things. If the dreamer is female and dreams that she is marrying a man of the cloth it says that the man she loves does not return her affection and that she will either die a spinster or marry for the sake of it. Dour Presbyterian ministers may suggest that change of an unpleasant nature is in the air and that that may necessitate an equally unpleasant journey. If the minister is preaching, then dreamer beware for someone you know will try to tempt you off the path of righteousness! And to dream that you are a minister suggests that you have your eyes on someone else's property and will be quite unscrupulous in getting it.

● ●

Waiters and **waitresses**, seen in dreams, mean different things depending on if the dreamer is doing the waiting or being waited on. If it's the former, then we are acknowledging an awareness of our ability to care for other people. If it's the latter, then it's the dreamer who is looking for that care.

Workshops signify that powerful enemies are working against you and that to win over them you will have to go to undreamed of lengths.

A Motion of Dreams

The way we move in dreams tells us a huge amount about how we see ourselves and to what degree we accept that insight. If we see ourselves moving quickly, that could mean that we know that there is a necessity to make a change of some sort in our lives and we are ready, if not willing to make it. If on the other hand we are being moved, the meaning may be that we feel that we are being forced to accept changes that we are very reluctant to make. If we are conscious of movement, then we may be being given choices in some aspects of our lives – going forwards seems to indicate that we accept our abilities and are willing to make the most of them on our onward path through life. Moving backwards suggests that we are in a situation of our own making from which we want to withdraw. Moving sideways suggests that we are intentionally about to avoid getting into a situation. That said ...

Crawling suggests that the dreamer is aware that things are not going particularly well in life. If the hands and knees are hurting, this is a sign that the dreamer expects that some sort of humiliation lies ahead. If the dream involves crawling over a rough area, then there

● ●

is an increasing awareness that opportunities are not being grasped and are slipping through the dreamer's fingers. If the dreamer is a woman, then deep down she may know that her behaviour is causing her lover to have some doubts about how seriously she sees their relationship. And if the dreamer is crawling through mud, friends might well think that the dreamer's conduct, particularly in business matters, is a cause for concern.

Exercise and dreams of physical accomplishment suggest well being, particularly when seen enjoyed as a group activity. If the dreamer sees himself in a state of physical exhaustion at the end of the dream then there is an active social life coming up. But as with so many dreams, nothing is fixed in stone, and dreams featuring exercise can also herald problems, particularly within the family or in business affairs that have yet to be resolved.

Exploration in general, when the dreamer sees himself setting out to discover new worlds, can only be good. But struggling upriver, hacking one's way through dense jungle can herald a jungle of problems. At best, the dreamer is going to break through what is holding him back in life: at worst, he is going to be stuck where he is for some time – maybe forever. As someone said, playing Tarzan has its hazards, but who knows – Jane might be about to make her presence known.

Falling is one of the most basic of dreams. Most falls are falls without end, which make such dreams difficult to interpret. That said, almost every dream interpreter has tried! Being in freefall can indicate breaking away from some problematic condition or relationship. It can also indicate that the clouds of misfortune are gathering on the horizon. If the dream-fall does have a conclusion and you hit earth, then you can expect real problems.

Flying is usually to do with sex and sexuality, perhaps a signal that we are ready to shake off inhibitions and be ourselves. On a less sexual level, to be flying upwards means that we are ready to move up to a more spiritual level in our lives, while to be going down is to be trying to come to terms with the darker side of our subconcious mind.

Floating was also traditionally thought (well, according to Freud at least) to be concerned with sexuality, but others see it as a sign that we feel restricted and our subconscious is telling us that we feel a deep need for more freedom in our lives, not necessarily just in matters sexual. It may signify that we are willing to put ourselves in the lap of the gods and are willing to be swept along by the tide of events. On the other hand, it may indicate that we know that we need to think more carefully about our actions and how they affect other people.

Jumping, like all repetitive dream movements, suggests conversely that it's time to stand still and take stock of where we are in life and what we are doing with the opportunities that have so far presented themselves. If we see ourselves as jumping upwards to get to a higher level, then we are trying to achieve something in real life that deep down we know that at best might mean a great deal of hard work, and at worst may be impossible to get to, no matter how hard we strive. Jumping downwards on to the level below can indicate an awareness that it's time to start looking at talents that may lie unearthed. Jumping up and down like a hyperactive child has two, opposite, meanings. On the one hand, it can indicate that happy times lie ahead. On the other hand, it could mean that frustration in all its many guises lies ahead. If the dream concerns jumping down from a wall, then be canny in business or what seemed to be a good investment might prove costly. Jumping over an obstacle and clearing it, suggests success all round, but if there's a fall, then life may be about to take a turn for the worse. If the dreamer is a woman and she sees herself jumping over something successfully then, after clearing many obstacles, maybe parental opposition, she will achieve her heart's desire.

Rocking is a sign that the dreamer seeks the comfort of childhood and wants to enjoy it for a while before taking stock and moving on. It is often experienced by people who are presented with unexpected challenges that they know are achievable but that they are unwilling to face because of the disruption they may cause.

Sliding is a sign that the path to true love will not run smoothly as promises will be broken, indeed the dreamer may be aware that they already have been. To see yourself sliding down a grass-covered hill warns that the dreamer is susceptible to flattery and that this may cause him or her to enter a business partnership that may result in significant losses.

Swimming has a variety of meanings because in the language of dreams, water is symbolic of our emotional life. If we see ourselves swimming against the current, then we are probably aware that we are doing something or acting in a fashion that is against our own nature. Swimming in crystal clear water is an indication that we have done something of which we

• •

are deeply ashamed and that we have a deep-seated desire to be cleansed of it. If the water is dark, then depression might be about to cloud our lives.

Walking is an indication that we want to move forward, to explore life and all that it offers. If we are walking purposefully then we know where we are going but if we are ambling aimlessly, then we are being told that it's time to create goals for ourselves. If we are enjoying a pleasant walk in the countryside, then deep down we wish to return to the state of innocence in which we were so happy as children. If we see ourselves as using a walking stick, then we are acknowledging our need for the support of others. A pleasant stroll through the countryside says that separation from good friends will be a cause of great unhappiness but that there may be compensation in that business affairs will bloom. But if the walk takes us through rough terrain then tangled business affairs will cause misunderstandings that will turn warm friends to indifferent acquaintances.

A Garden of Dreams

Dreams of plants of all sorts – trees, flowers, fruit, crops, anything, in fact that grows – take root in our dreams, grow and bloom, and hold all sorts of meanings for the sleeper.

Gardens in general represent the inner person, the feelings, instincts and beliefs that take root and grow deep within the dreamer. A badly kept garden may indicate that the dreamer sees him or herself as suffering from indecision and lack of purpose, unwilling to plant seeds that will germinate and take root in all aspects of life. Some would say that a garden dreamed of as suffering from neglect, indicates that deep down the dreamer is aware that neglect has been allowed to creep into all aspects of life. On the other hand, a tidy garden with well-manicured lawns and well-kept flowerbeds suggests confidence that plans laid will come to happy fruition, having been laid by a well-ordered but perhaps over-controlled mind.

Similarly, a well-tended field, full of ripening crops denotes certain prosperity in the future, founded on well-thought-out schemes, while a barren one denotes disappointment.

A-Z OF DREAMS

● ●

There are hundreds of thousands of individual plants, trees, flowers, fruits and other ingredients in Nature's larder, many of which have their own significance to the dreamer. There are too many to mention individually here, but hopefully those that are mentioned will help those who seek to give meaning to their dreams.

Acacia flowers, sacred to the Ancient Egyptians, signify an erotic encounter is on the horizon, according to Freud. But in gypsy folklore, which dates back centuries before the Austrian psychologist turned his attention to dreams and dreamers, they signify rest and tranquillity.

Acorns are a symbol of great growth potential, be it spiritual, physical or mental – hardly surprising when one considers that the mighty oak grows from a single acorn. It can denote that health and happiness are about to take root in the dreamer's life, and if he is single, a long and happy marriage awaits.

Almond trees, indeed trees of any kind, had erotic significance to Freud, but other analysts associate this nut-bearing tree with upcoming success. To dream of eating an almond suggests that the dreamer is about

• •

to enjoy travelling to foreign lands in the not-too-distant future. But if the almond is bitter, the journey will not be a happy one.

Apples, in spite of their notorious history involving nothing less than the downfall of man and expulsion from the Garden of Eden, are generally regarded as fortuitous in dreams. Walking through apple trees (also see **Orchards**) can indicate fruitfulness and since medieval times have been seen as suggesting a time of good harvest, which today can mean success in business. If, however, there are many fallen apples and you inadvertently walk upon them, that promise is compromised. One source suggests that if you dream of eating a sweet apple you are due for an unspecified happy event. A sour apple suggests exactly the opposite. To dream of an apple tree means that good news is about to drop through the letter box, but only if the tree is alive and flourishing. If it's dead, then beware the postman's tread, for bad tidings are in his bag.

Bamboo featuring in dreams, means that a dispute of some sort is about to shoot through your family circle, causing dissent. Often the finger of guilt will point at the dreamer as being the cause of this dissent.

A-Z OF DREAMS

●●●●●●●●●●●●●●●●●●●●●●●●●●●●●●●●●●●●●●

Bananas are unwelcome in the symbolism of dreams. Eating them suggests that misfortune is about to trip the dreamer up.

Barley fields may beckon the rural rambler, but to dream of walking through them suggests that the seeds of something sown in the past are about to be harvested and that the outcome will not be particularly pleasant.

Beans are not welcome additions to the vocabulary of the language of dreams. To dream that you are eating them augurs ill health is in the wind. To see them growing in the pod suggests that the clouds of contentious arguments are on the horizon and about to be blown in.

Brambles or **briars** suggest that the dreamer is desperately seeking love but that the current object of his attraction is unattainable and always will be.

Cabbages seen growing in the fields signify that a long, healthy life stretches ahead of the dreamer. But if the dreamer sees himself eating them sorrow will soon be experienced, loss will be felt and illness is about to point its finger at the dreamer and beckon him to its side.

• •

Cedar trees with their well-known shape and height, distinctive perfume and healing qualities should, if things were what they seem on the dream landscape, denote that happiness, joy and peace are about to wrap themselves round the dreams. And for once, the obvious is the actual.

Cherries, one of the sweetest of summer fruits, bring two sweet meanings to the dreamer. And one sour one. Seeing them on the branch points to a healthy, fertile life ahead. Eating them denotes a lucky love life. But if the cherries are being gathered, then a woman of the dreamer's acquaintance has deception on her mind.

Cornfields and **corn** (also see **Oats**) have come down to us from the ancient Greek myths as the greatest fertility symbol. People literally went to Hell and back to protect its potency. All dreams of corn are good. Walking through a field of corn suggests a happy meeting at the other side. The very sight of large ears of corn signifies good news, whilst eating a stalk of corn (an unlikely dream in modern times) presages a happy union. In the Bible, Joseph dreamed that the corn sheaves he and his brothers were making bowed down and worshipped him. When he suggested on waking that his brothers do likewise the antagonism this resulted in eventually saw his siblings sell him into slavery! *Caveat dreamers!*

Daffodils, the happy heralds of spring, indicate that good things are about to bloom in the dreamer's life, especially in health matters. Sunshine will flood into every corner, spreading warmth and perhaps bringing wealth in its wake.

Daisies may be a nightmare for gardeners in search of the perfect lawn, but if they show their pretty heads in spring or summer dreams they suggest that a true lover is about to present him or herself. Sadly, if daisies show themselves in winter or autumn dreams, the looming lover will turn out to be wearing his heart on his sleeve.

Dandelions warn that someone you trust and who may be working with you on a project close to *your* heart, has perfidiousness inscribed on *his.*

Dates, in the recent past in northern European countries, part of the traditional contents of a child's Christmas stocking have a contradictory meaning to the dreamer. Common to both is that a person of the opposite sex is about to loom large. But while he or she may turn out to be a strong admirer, he or she is just as likely to turn out to be a powerful enemy!

Elderberries, the fruit of a tree sacred to those who follow the pagan path, suggest that news of a pleasant nature will soon reach the dreamer's ears. It may be the successful conclusion of a wealth-bearing venture or that marriage plans are about to accelerate.

Farms are among the oldest dreams recorded, which is not surprising as for most of our time on the planet we have been a self-sufficient rural economy. The whims of the heavens that could produce desperate famine or great plenty have defined our lives. Think of Ancient Egypt (where many of the first dreams were recorded) and the importance of the rise and fall of the River Nile. In more recent times farms have had rather a surface meaning of productivity and growth, making new friends and of generally prospering. This held true in America even in the 1930s when whole swathes of the country became a dustbowl as recorded by John Steinbeck in his great novel *The Grapes of Wrath*. The land is so much part of us. Now dreaming of farming suggests harking back to the past. Certainly not of prosperity in the future.

• •

Figs may be a pleasure to eat, but to dream of eating them suggests that the clouds of ill-fortune may be looming. They may bring loss of actual fortune or they may bring shame with them. If the dream is dreamt when the fruit is not in season, then the clouds may be black – funeral black, in fact!

Flowers can be difficult to define when they feature in dreams. They have great individual meanings in astrology, aromatherapy and other New Age studies, but in dreams they seem to merge into one great bouquet. Obvious interpretations involve romance, but this is far too easy. Wild flowers provide the best omens, often suggesting impending sexual encounters. If these don't happen they still suggest only pleasant adventures. Generally speaking – if one can talk generalities in the dream context – flowers are symbolic of beauty, love and tenderness. Of course, they have sexual connotations: a blossoming flower is symbolic of female genitalia, a bud of the male sexual organ. If the flowers dreamed of are in season, joy may be about to flood into the dreamer's life, *unless* the flowers are white in which case the joy may be short lived, or yellow, which presages difficulties of some sort, or red – in which case death may be about to shroud a loved one.

● ●

Gooseberries are an ancient symbol of reproduction and fertility and in dreams signify that plans conceived at the time of the dream will come to a fruitful conclusion.

Grapes have played such a large part in creating the psyche of the people through success and calamity that every grape-growing country has its own mythology of the grape. A glorious harvest in prospect could be ruined overnight by a flash storm, so it is no surprise that the people of Italy, France and neighbouring vine-growing countries had nightmares. Being surrounded by a flourishing vineyard meant long life, but eating them meant problems. They should only be drunk! It is reported that the Romans associated white grapes with victory (and they had a few) while black grapes suggested opposition. In recent years stories have emerged from Australia that if a woman dreams of grapes she has a passionate relationship on the horizon. It is too early to decide if this is a marketing gimmick.

Grass features in our dreams as often as it features in the landscape of our lives. To see oneself walking through a grassy meadow points to burgeoning happiness and good fortune. But if the dreamer is eating grass, there may be sickness and sorrow ahead. And misfortune of some kind is indicated if the grass dreamed of is dead or withered.

Hawthorn trees used to be a common feature of the rural landscape: sadly there are fewer dancing on the horizon nowadays. But this once-constant feature of the countryside continues to denote constancy in one's life.

Heather, as all those who have been importuned to buy a sprig of 'lucky' heather will be aware, has a long and glorious history. Earliest recorded dreams of this wild plant that infests Scotland are from the fourteenth century and, like so many dreams, suggest a partnership around the next corner. As a lot of the heather now comes from the Netherlands we think this dream has had its moment.

Hedges were seen by Freud as a sign that the dreamer had a deep-rooted fear of sex, but to other interpreters, a thick, green hedge was a sign that long-lasting prosperity was in the offing. But if the hedge is scraggy and thorny, then the way ahead is fraught with danger and difficulty.

Herbs such as rosemary and thyme, sage and parsley, all have long literary allusions. However, in the

• •

dream world they tend to be bunched together. They can indicate a long life (especially in North American lore) or a long journey. Some middle European sources suggest that they can indicate a cure if there is a problem in the family, but it is advisable not to take such omens seriously. Your doctor or alternative medicine practitioner is possibly a better bet. To dream of poisonous herbs, such as henbane or hemlock denotes danger down the path, but herbs which are used to beneficial purpose are usually regarded as a good sign.

Holly, with its luminous green leaves and bright red berries is a portent of good things to come, but, as suggested by the thorny leaves, there may be some difficulties in achieving them.

Hyacinth, the delightful blooms that lend their heady fragrance to our lives, lend sweet things to our dreams, too, telling us that riches are about to waft in our direction.

Ivy is one of the most prolific and persistent plants – try killing it or stopping it overgrowing a wall or tree! Its persistence, if you are observing it in your dream, suggests personal growth, business success and long life. As with so many dreams there can be a dark side.

A-Z OF DREAMS

If you become entangled with ivy, personal relationships are endangered and you may find yourself entangled with someone you simply cannot shake off. Ivy, like willow or gold-tipped pfitzer, is often associated with graveyards with gloomy overtones. But as with so many dreams, opposites rule. 'O Death, where is thy sting?' Think positive.

Jasmine, according to Romany lore foretells of love, true love, about to smile on those in search of it. Those who have already been hit by Cupid's arrows, can expect their love to intensify if this fragrant flower perfumes their dreams.

Jungles (or heavy undergrowth) and being lost in them feature in many recurring dreams. It seems obvious to think that entanglement with tendrils and branches suggests battling against the odds, personal and financial. But it is surprising how often people break through with almost Tarzan-like facilities, jumping from branch to branch until light is in sight. It has been reported that this is also a metaphor for breaking free from some restraints, perhaps seeking new work experiences.

● ●

Juniper, the plant that lends its flavour to gin, intoxicates the lives of those who dream about cutting a juniper bush, presaging as it does good luck. But if the dream is of eating juniper berries, then take this as a warning that newly formed associations may turn out to be unwise.

Laurel was the plant that lent its leaves to the victor's crown in Classical times. It is appropriate then that if it features in a dream it signifies that victory is the dreamer's in any current or upcoming contest, and that the victory will be a particularly pleasurable one.

Leaves are not unconnected with previously explained **Ivy** and **Jungles**. This is another 'nature' dream. Green leaves presage growth, which equals good health, prosperity and a prospective vigorous love life. Brown leaves, perhaps walking through a carpet of them, mean just the opposite almost to the point of death. Walking through a rain of falling leaves can be positive as it suggests that you should stop wasting parts of your life, personal or business.

Lemons feature in dreams that are often as sharp as the fruits themselves. A healthy lemon tree with lots of fruits and rich foliage equals jealousy, usually misplaced. Eating lemons suggests eating one's words, or some other humiliation. In Middle Eastern culture to dream of dried lemons (not a common dream) means divorce or separation. Green lemons, not that common north of the Mediterranean, also bode ill.

Lentils are not commonly dreamt about in northern countries, but are starting to become more evident as they appear on international menus. They don't suggest anything good anyway. As they are dried, they often suggest barren relationships and unhealthy surroundings. But within their dried exterior there is goodness which can suggest that a difficult relationship might be worth sticking with. Things may turn out all right.

Lettuce dreamed about in any of its many varieties has been recorded over the years as being connected with embarrassment which turns out well, providing you see it growing. Eating it is a different matter. It can engender jealousy and envy. The green connection? Sowing lettuce, first reported in the early 1900s, and not a common activity, denotes early sickness and death. Buying lettuce suggests you will be the architect of your own downfall. Avoid lettuce.

Lilies, elegant symbols of chastity, purity and innocence, suggest that happiness will soon bloom in the dreamer's life and that that happiness will be achieved through virtue. To dream of lily of the valley tells the dreamer that to achieve happiness, he or she should act with humility. Water lilies foretell that regeneration in some form is in the offing. Lotus lilies herald a new birth and a long life, while tiger lilies warn the dreamer that temptation of some sort, probably wealth, will be put in his path.

Limes are much the same as lemons in a dream dictionary. They are not good news, as if you are ill you are not going to get much better in the near future.

Maple, the national emblem of Canada and provider of the syrup enjoyed in much of North America, tells that comfort and happiness will soon pour and spread through the dreamer's life.

Marigolds symbolize that a new love will prove to be long-lasting and constant. A marriage in the offing will be long and happy. And if that isn't enough this generous flower promises advancement in career matters and rich rewards coming the dreamer's way.

Melons, with their soft flesh and mouthwatering juiciness do not feature much on the canvas of dreams. But on the rare occasions that they do, and if the dreamer is sick, then the fruit is a happy symbol, suggesting that good health will soon be restored.

Mistletoe, sacred to Pagans, Druids and followers of New Age ways of life, and under sprigs of which revellers kiss at Christmas, blesses dreamers with good fortune and promises of ongoing good health.

Moss clings to the rocks on which it spreads, and if it features in a dream, it suggests that wealth will spread in the dreamer's direction and that it will cling to him or her.

Mushrooms, cultivated as they are in the dark and damp, denote unhealthy desires from sexual to financial matters. Early reports suggest that anything acquired on either of these fronts will be lost through profligacy. Dreaming of eating them has, since the late 1800s, suggested, to quote one dream interpreter, 'humiliation and disgraceful love', and to paraphrase the words of another, death to those who dream of eating this fungus.

● ●

Nettles, despite their obvious sting, can prove beneficial if you dream that you are walking through them without being stung, for then prosperity beckons. If you are stung you are going to make someone, perhaps a partner, unhappy. Generally nettles are a warning to be stringent with your means. Nettle dreams go back a long way as it can be forgotten that they were the source of both food and drink in the Middle Ages. They are currently coming back into fashion, so there may be more nettle dreams.

Nuts. Gathering nuts (in May?) has good auguries, not unconnected with amorous adventures. These usually involve new partnerships, which does not do much if you are currently in a happy relationship. Fortunately these same signs can be interpreted as an aid to prosperity in financial matters.

Oak. Some of the oldest recorded dreams involve oak trees, inevitably connected to England. They are associated with security, emotional and financial. A tree full of acorns is the greatest symbol of increase, profusion and possibly an inheritance. But beware blasted oaks and falling leaves, which suggest exactly the opposite. Fanciful dreams of lovers under oaks, from the Middle Ages, suggest early marriage.

A-Z OF DREAMS

Oats. These do not feature greatly in dreams today but they were a mainstay of the diet when dreams were first recorded and could decide whether or not an agrarian community (most) and its livestock could make it through a difficult winter. In general, they are a good sign suggesting a good harvest in the fields and at the hearth.

Olives. These do not loom large in northern culture, but should you dream of collecting them (usually with a band of jolly friends) business is going to prosper. Eating them, or even using their precious oil, tells of conviviality. A good time is going to be had by all. Accidentally smashing a bottle of oil is not as disastrous as it sounds. Possible small disappointments. Nothing more.

Onions. They make your eyes water and have therefore been erroniously associated with sad events. Far from it. You are going to be very successful but, and there is always a but with dreams, they tell you to beware of spite and envy at your success. If you dream of eating them raw (not an everyday occurrence) you will ride over the opposition. Eating them cooked means only modest gains, but you are still on the winning side.

• •

Oranges. Seeing them, good. Eating them, bad. Some of the earliest dreams have been associated with them as they have been confused with the 'golden fruit' which Eve partook of (actually an apricot) and the golden apples from the Garden of the Hesperides. If you dream of a fine one so high on the tree that you cannot reach it, it means you will one day make a fine and lasting relationship. As recently as the 1800s, when death loomed much larger than today, eating an orange and spilling its luscious juice suggested an impending death in the family. Perhaps A.A. Milne was right when he wrote 'the only safe place to eat an orange is in the bath'.

Orchards. Strolling idyllically through an orchard with a partner is the greatest romantic image. But beware the fallen fruit. Remember the Garden of Eden. It is unlikely to happen to you, but one of the earliest dream interpreters warns 'if you see a hog eating fallen fruit you will lose all your property, particularly if you have not been honest in acquiring it'. If the orchard is full of trees heavy with fruit, that tells that the dreamer can expect a life of abundance. But if the trees are fruitless, then plans being laid will come to nothing and wealth already accrued may start to erode.

● ●

Palm trees. These provide an ideal image for aspiration and escape. Walking down an avenue of such is the road to new beginnings and not just a blissful holiday experience. Though perhaps these are the same two things. Recently a French writer suggested that they are heightened symbols of aspirations. But, not surprisingly, at almost the same time a British writer suggested that they symbolize the great height from which you could be let down by a friend.

Parsley (see **Herbs**). One of the most potent of herbs which in nature has long roots, said to go to the Devil and back. Such peristence pays off with good health and good fortune. The only drawback is that in the 1890s it was written that 'the fecundity produced may reduce the means to support the offspring'.

Parsnips. Surprisingly there are no recorded sexual connotations regarding this vegetable. In fact it is a better omen for trade than love.

Peaches. So luscious when awake, presage illness when in dreams, particularly where children are involved. Observing them growing prolifically is a better sign. You will prosper in your desired profession. Dried peaches, not exactly common, are a warning that colleagues may be conspiring against you.

Pears may be golden on the bough, but are not so in dreams. Eating them reduces chances of success and even means health problems. Just seeing them suggests that your aspirations can prove a mirage. Harvesting them seems so profitable at the time, but will be followed quickly by disappointment. Perhaps this mirrors reality. Pears rot quicker than most fruit. At least dreaming of preserving them suggests that you can take setbacks philosophically.

Peas at one time featured largely in dreams, no doubt because of their importance as a crop. Medieval peasants were not aware of Bird's Eye which has probably reduced their importance to our psyche. Curiously when canning was first invented, opening one can either revealed a lot of little problems or gave you momentary hope. Dreaming of dried peas (also see **Lentils**) suggests you are overstraining and as a result likely to decrease life's pleasures and wealth.

Pomegranates do not feature much in dreams these days but dreaming of them in Roman times was a symbol of wisdom and also meant that the dreamer was one who used his mind to enrich others. If given one you will be sensible, but sensual. If you actually eat it – watch out!

Poplar, once sacred to the Greek god Heracles, foretells that hopes will be fulfilled and that dreams of good things will come true. But only if the tree is green and is bursting with life. A withered poplar is a sad sight, and sad too will be the person who dreams of it, for disappointment will soon darken the skies.

Poppies blooming and bobbing their red petals in a cornfield are one of the delights of the countryside. Sadly they signify no delights for the dreamer, for they warn that ill health will soon afflict the dreamer or someone in the immediate family circle.

Potatoes are good omens as they have prolific flowers and leaves above ground whilst they are being equally, if not more, prolific underground. Digging or pulling them up denotes success in business and personal life. Small new potatoes, pulled fresh from the earth suggest great achievements. If you then cook them you will have pleasant employment, problem free. If you previously planted them your great desires have a good chance of being realized. The only small problem is that should you pull up some rotted ones (through overwatering, perhaps?) your pleasures might be diminished but not blighted.

Primroses may belong to a different family from poppies, but like them they carry a message that illness may soon strike and that whoever is afflicted may not survive.

Pumpkins should be welcomed in dreams, especially by those suffering from a lonely heart, for they tell that the dreamers will soon be surrounded by admirers and that one of them could well turn out to be 'the one'.

Rhubarb with its great leaves suggests a jungle and the glorious red stems are equally evocative. It grew in almost every garden not many years ago, but today is more likely to be harvested from supermarket shelves. Generally it is an omen of good, but to dream of cooking it (which you more or less have to) suggests argument and a break with a friend. Eating it has also been thought to suggest great unhappiness with your present work situation.

Rice is an omen of nothing but good. It means growth in every direction, work or personal relationships. At its most basic if you are a farmer your harvest will prosper, but on the more general canvas you are assured domestic bliss and increased wealth.

A-Z OF DREAMS

Rosemary (also see **Herbs**) was, according to Shakespeare, 'for remembrance' but in dreams it has connotations of sadness. Though it adds fragrance and taste to many real-life dishes, in dreams it bodes ill for relationships which, on the surface, may seem very happy.

Roses are probably one of the more obvious symbols of everyday life. Dream of them blooming beautifully and your life will follow suit – you may even succeed in a love quest you previously thought hopeless. Smelling heavy fragrance of rose suggests a future of complete pleasure. On the dark side, withered roses show a lack of relationships and white roses (perhaps because of their drained look – roses should be red) suggest impending illness.

Rye is not commonly dreamed of (also see **Cornfields** and **Oats**) as the rural economy does not loom large in lives today. But in times when it meant survival through a winter, to dream of rye meant great prosperity and a good future.

Salad may, in real life, be an essential part of a healthy diet but in dreams there are few other than bad omens. Eating it suggests illness, quarrels and

● ●

meeting disagreeable people. Inexplicable, but that is the way of dreams.

Straw, if seen in dreams burning, once a common scene in the countryside, suggests prosperity, but straightforward bales of straw suggest an empty life. If the dream concerns feeding your animals on straw, this suggests that the dreamer has not made sufficient provision for his or her nearest and dearest.

Sycamore's meaning depends on the marital state of the dreamer. For a single person to dream of this proud tree signifies that marriage is on the horizon, or if not marriage then a lifelong commitment to another. But if the dreamer is already married, the sycamore suggests that the green-eyed monster of jealousy will soon turn his gaze in the dreamer's direction.

Tamarind trees, native as they are to tropical climes, do not appear very often in the dreams of those who live in cooler parts of the world. If they do, then they cast themselves in the role of weather forecaster, for they mean that rain is about to blow in. On a non-meteorological level they warn that a woman will bring trouble into the dreamer's life.

● ●

Toadstools appear overnight in fields and gardens. When they appear in dreams they signify that the dreamer is due sudden elevation in career matters.

Tomatoes, curiously, were once thought of as toxic and dangerous to eat. That belief has long since fallen off the vine and today, to dream that one is eating tomatoes, is a sign that happiness is about to appear, but like the fruit itself which rots after a few days, the happiness will be short-lived.

Trees represent so many aspects of our lives that it is hardly surprising that they have a wide variety of meanings when they root, shoot, bud, grow and die in our dreams. And so many trees have their own meanings that to mention them all would result in a book with many more pages than this. To be brief, a tree with new foliage appearing, means your greatest hopes are on the verge of consummation. Climbing trees is a too obvious simile for aspiring to better things. Cutting one down or pulling it up by the roots shows a wasting of your energies. Falling leaves are symbolic of what we have or hope to cast off, while the fruits of the tree represent what we have created in life. A tree seen growing, mirrors a subconscious desire for growth, in the physical, emotional or psychological area. A dead tree may foretell that the

• •

grim reaper is about to wield his scythe, or that
something we value will pass from our lives. To dream
of branches laden with fruit and bright with green
leaves, is a portent of wealth and the opportunity to
spend time with friends. But if the branches are barren,
there is likely to be bad news of long-lost friends.
Withered leaves tell that hopes will rise only to be
dashed almost immediately, and if the dreamer is a
young woman then marital happiness may evade her –
forever. Blossom covered trees promise prosperity
while to see roots spreading warns of declining health
and a shrinking business. (Also see individual trees.)

Vegetables being eaten in dreams, generally
suggests a quirk of unexpected luck. This can be
Janus-faced. You might think you are on the verge of
great success and it collapses and vice-versa. Dreams
of rotten vegetables are an unmitigated disaster.

Vines are generally a sign of success, happiness and
great health. Visiting a vineyard suggests an auspicious
love-making partnership. But if anything is seen
withering on the vine, beware. Business schemes, in
particular, are likely to fail.

A-Z OF DREAMS

●●●●●●●●●●●●●●●●●●●●●●●●●●●●●●●●●●●●

Walnuts are good and bad in equal quantities. A fresh nut when opened suggests great happiness and a favourable life. A decayed nut tells you that your great expectations will end in nothing.

Yew trees, sacred to the Romans and used by British archers to fashion their bows, suggest that considerable wealth is about to line the dreamer's coffers. The wealth may walk hand in hand with honours of some sort being showered on the dreamer.

A Wardful of Dreams

No matter how kind and friendly are the doctors and nurses who look after us when we are sick, and no matter how rarely we have to go and see them, we all have a deep subconscious fear of ill health. This, naturally spills into our dream world – where, as usual, all is not always as it seems. Not always!

Ambulances seen or heard with their sirens blaring, their lights blazing and weaving their way through traffic are not to be welcomed for they bring bad luck and misfortune in their wake. And if the dreamer is inside one, then illness could soon strike.

Amputations are a warning to watch out, for things could be about to take a turn for the worse. Losing part of a limb suggests that prestige, perhaps on the work front, is about to suffer through no fault of the dreamer, but even so to restore the loss of reputation could be quite a challenge. To have an entire arm or leg cut off is a sign that there's a downturn ahead on the job front, especially for the self-employed or those in trade or business. Amputations have their own, special significance for sailors, warning them that

• •

choppy waters are in the offing as a result of which property will be lost.

Anaesthetics suggest that the dreamer realizes that he has been burying his head ostrich-like in the sand about some overpowering emotion and that now is the time to stare it straight in the face and come to terms with it. It can also indicate a death, perhaps not a physical one, but of a part of oneself the uselessness of which is now causing problems.

Bandages wind their way into our dreams with surprising frequency! If dreamers see themselves being bandaged, then recent emotional upsets are about to be soothed. If the bandage is slipping off, it's time to look to the responsibilities that have been voluntarily assumed as acquaintances think that the dreamer is being slipshod in their administration.

Bed wetting indicates that the dreamer is increasingly anxious over things that are out of his or her control, perhaps in matters regarding sexuality. It can also say that the dreamer is afraid that he has been charged by society with some sort of improper conduct and has been found guilty without having been given the opportunity of speaking in his own defence. Wetting the bed can also suggest that the dreamer wants to shrug off the shackles of convention and claim the freedom to express him or herself in a totally unexpected way. There is another meaning of course ...

Burns signify good news is on the way. If it is the feet that are burned then the word 'impossible' does not exist in your vocabulary – at least in the immediate future. If you are in good health, things won't change. But if you are sick, you will soon be up and about again.

Cancer, which many of us think is a modern-day problem, is not. It has been afflicting people for centuries and has made its presence felt in dreams for just as long. To dream that one has cancer is not a portent of ill health, but it does warn that people one loves might for no apparent reason be about to become unusually quarrelsome. And to the businessman the same dream can mean that cost-cutting measures might have to be seriously considered. To dream that cancer has been successfully treated is a sign that an upturn in the dreamer's own business or in his or her employer's will be reflected in a salary rise or bonus being paid.

Castration suggests that the dreamer is increasingly aware that his sexual balance is out of

● ●

kilter and it's time to bring the masculine and feminine sides of the personality back into harmony with each other. It can also indicate a deeply felt disgust of the sexual act and a desire to revert to the sexually innocent days of childhood.

Coughing serves as a warning to take a little more care than usual regarding health matters. But even if illness does make itself felt, it won't last for long and you will soon be back on your feet. If you hear someone else cough you may be about to change environment – not necessarily for the better. If the cough is more of a bronchial wheeze, then sickness of someone close to you may be about to make you change your plans. And if it is a consumptive rasping for breath, stick to the safety of old friends no matter how tempting it may be to seek the pleasures that new friends may offer.

Crutches are an acknowledgement either that someone is looking to the dreamer for support or the dreamer is looking for someone to give him or her the prop-up that is needed in emotional rather than financial matters. They can also suggest that the dreamer is increasingly dissatisfied and disenchanted with other people's shortcomings and weaknesses. And lastly, that the dreamer is increasingly aware that he or she is becoming too dependent on outside stimuli such as drugs, tobacco or alcohol.

Death is perhaps one of the most common subjects of dreams – whether it be the dreamer or another person who is seen to shuffle off the coils of mortal life. To dream of seeing a member of the family dead is a warning that the dreamer's increasingly dissolute way of life is being talked about among relations and friends. Such dreams are often followed by disappointment of some sort. If, in the dream, the death is heard about rather than seen, then bad news is on its way.

Drugs, when they appear in dreams, indicate that we have a problem that needs the help of an outside source before we can either solve it completely or at least come to terms with it. If we see ourselves taking drugs, then we are admitting that we have lost control of something, probably in our private lives, and have no idea how to put ourselves back in the driving seat. To have been given drugs and to see ourselves reacting badly indicates that we have a deep-seated fear of madness, while to be seen struggling against being given drugs says that we may have to face up to accepting an unpalatable truth.

A-Z OF DREAMS

●●●●●●●●●●●●●●●●●●●●●●●●●●●●●●●●●●●●●

Dying is a warning that someone who gave the
dreamer a leg up in business or career matters is
about to change position and start to plot to bring
about the dreamer's downfall. To see others die in a
dream portends bad luck either to the dreamer or to a
friend or relative. Dreaming of an imminent death says
that it's time the dreamer realized that paying attention
to detail would pay dividends: in fact, if the warning is
ignored the results could be disastrous. Dreams that
death is just around the corner can also herald a bout
of ill health. The only mildly good thing about dreams of
death is if the dead or dying are animal rather than
human, for to dream of the last moment of a wild
animal says that the dreamer will escape being
enveloped in some sort of evil. If the doomed beast is
a pet, then dreamer beware! Bad luck beckons – not
very bad luck, but bad luck all the same.

Fainting is a warning that illness may be about to
hit your family or that you may receive bad news
about someone you haven't heard from for some time.
If the dreamer is a woman and she sees herself falling
into a deep faint, then she should mend her ways
because her carelessness might well be about to be
the cause of a deep disappointment. Fainting in a
dream can also indicate that someone you trust is
about to let you down.

Gout warns that a relative, not a necessarily a close one, is going to irritate the dreamer and may be the cause of him suffering a substantial loss of some kind: not an especially significant one, but a loss is a loss.

Hospitals are good news for the dreamer, not so good for those he or she knows! When dreamers see themselves as being patients in hospital, then there may well be an epidemic of some sort about to sweep the country. The dreamer will not be affected by it: the people he or she knows will not be so lucky. For people to dream that they are visiting friends or relatives in hospitals is an indication that sad news about an absent friend will soon be heard. To be seen leaving a hospital, having been confined there, suggests that the dreamer will be worried by the escapades of enemies, but that he or she will gain the upper hand and send them packing, licking their wounds.

Itches, if it is the dreamer who is affected, warn that you will stand accused of something of which you are innocent, but you will have some difficulty proving it. For a woman to dream that she is itching suggests that she has not chosen her companions wisely and she is in danger of being tempted to fall into dissolute ways. To see someone else obviously suffering from an itch suggests that plans you were laying for a pleasant purpose will go awry.

Limping is a warning that something you have been looking forward to for some time will be marred by an unexpected worry. To dream that someone else is limping, tells you that a friend will do something in all innocence that will cause you to take great offence.

Measles say that it's time to relax for if you become over-anxious, particularly about business affairs, your health could suffer.

Medicine's meaning depends on the medicine's taste! If it is sweet then there's trouble in store, but the dreamer will survive and grow in stature as a result. If on the other hand, the medicine tastes foul, then serious illness threatens, or if it doesn't materialize the alternative is just as worrying – sorrow and loss, deep sorrow and significant loss. For a dreamer to administer medicine is a sign that someone who trusts you is about to be disappointed in you.

Numbness can signify that a bout of mild ill health may be about to lay the dreamer low. It may be little more than a vague feeling of being under the weather.

● ●

Nurses seen in the house suggest that the dreamer is concerned about their own health or that of someone close. If the nurse is a resident rather than a visitor, then an upcoming and much-looked-forward-to visit from friends will not go according to plan. In fact, if the friendship survives you'll be lucky. If, on the other hand, the nurse is being waved off, then good health is presaged. To see oneself in nurse's uniform, tending the sick, says that the dreamer will rise in the esteem of friends and employers. If, in the dream, the dreamer leaves the patient to attend to other matters then an acquaintance could be about to do their damnedest to persuade the dreamer to do something deceitful or that goes against the grain.

Ointments soothe our cuts and grazes in real life and they bring good news in our dream world, too, for they say that new friendships are about to be formed and that they will be long lasting and very advantageous to both parties. If the dreamer is a woman and she sees herself making an ointment, she is being given advance notice that she will soon be in a position to be in complete command of her own destiny in career matters and in affairs of the heart.

A-Z OF DREAMS

Paralysis has meanings for businessmen and for lovers. For the former to dream of being paralysed is a sign that a downturn in the business cycle may affect them more than their rivals. To those in love, the same dream indicates that things will not go smoothly – indeed the romance might well be heading for the rocks.

Pills being taken by dreamers foretell that more responsibility will be offered to them, but they will find the offer hard to swallow as they will soon realize that responsibility comes at a price. To be seen administering pills to others is a warning that others seem to be seeing you in a disagreeable light.

Pimples can represent blemishes in our character, which we know will have to be dealt with – sometime! They can also represent that although we know we are being negative, we don't seem to be able to do much about it. On another level, pimples tell the dreamer that he or she is far too concerned with trifling matters and that it's time to try to get the broader picture into perspective. To see others with pimply skin suggests that something another does or says will put brakes on the dreamer's rise up the ladder of career success, for a while at least. If the dreamer is a woman and she sees herself as being so pimply that people shun her, then she may have to mend her ways if she is to escape the wagging tongues of others in her immediate social circle.

Pulses serve as a dream warning to take care of yourself, unless the dreamer is taking the pulse of another rather than having their own one measured. If it is the latter case, then the dreamer is being warned that there has been a bit of overindulgence and that it's time to slow down not just for the body's sake, but for the reputation, too.

Quinine, the traditional anti-malaria treatment and indispensable ingredient of tonic water, does occasionally feature in dreams and when it does it heralds that a spell of happiness lies ahead. To dream that it is being swallowed, the meaning is threefold – an improvement in health, a boost to energy levels and, if these weren't enough, new friends, who will prove to be extremely generous.

Resuscitation has two meanings, depending on who is being resuscitated and who is doing the resuscitation. If it is the dreamer who is at the receiving end, then significant financial losses could be about to make themselves felt, but the effect will be temporary. There's good news if the dreamer is resuscitating another, for new friendships are about to be forged

● ●

and not only will they be enjoyable in themselves, they will enhance the dreamer's reputation – and maybe boost earnings.

Sores portend that illness will cause you considerable financial loss and may affect your mental balance for a short time. If the dream concerns dressing a sore, then your own dreams and desires will be given second place to the pleasures of a third party.

Stings warn that your happiness is about to be pierced by an unexpected tragic event.

Stretchers carry their own message – and it's not a particularly pleasant one. To see oneself stretcher borne means that you will soon be asked to undertake some task or accept a job that is distasteful, but that you will have no option but to grin and bear it! And to see a stretcher is a harbinger of bad news – not tragic or deeply upsetting, just mildly disagreeable.

Surgeons seen wielding the scalpel, suggest that the dreamer has business enemies who are plotting to get their own way at the dreamer's expense. For a woman to see herself on the surgeon's table is a warning that a bout of ill health is about to hit her.

Surgical instruments say that a friend may be about to cause concern by appearing to withdraw the hand of companionship and to be remote for no reason that the dreamer can think of.

Swellings dreamed of are a good sign in that they say that the dreamer will build a substantial fortune by working hard. But self-importance will inflate the dreamer's ego and stop him or her enjoying their good fortune.

Syringes warn that bad news about a relative's health is on the way. But before you pack the black tie and set off for the funeral, relax, for it will prove to be a false alarm and whoever has been sick will be well on the road to recovery even before the bad news is received. If the syringe is broken, then what might appear to be trifling little mistakes at work will cause a ripple effect that will have totally unexpected ramifications.

Thermometers warn that disharmony might be about to make itself felt at home and spill over into the office as well. If the thermometer is not working, then a bout of annoying rather than serious ill health could be about to afflict the dreamer. If the mercury is on the way down, the work front could be about to present a few

• •

problems, but if it is rising, then you are about to shrug
off bad luck and experience a spell of good fortune.

Trusses are unusual dream symbols, but they have
been reported from time to time, especially among the
elderly to whom they presage an unpredictable,
perhaps inequitable, financial future.

Vaccination to the male dreamer says to him that
he is too susceptible to the charm of ambitious
females who will unscrupulously use him for their own
ends. For both sexes to dream that they are
vaccinating others suggests that no matter where the
dreamers look to find happiness and contentment,
these will be constantly elusive. And for a young
woman to see herself being vaccinated in the leg,
means she should keep her sense of smell alert for the
whiff of treachery in the air.

Vomiting says that a scandal of some sort may be
about to engulf the dreamer. But if it doesn't appear
the dreamer cannot relax, for there's just a chance that
he will come down with some sort of affliction that
could leave him temporarily disabled. The latter is more
likely if there is blood in the vomit. Blood-flecked sick
also warns that children are going to be more than a
handful and will cause heartache after heartache,

• •

leaving the dreamer more than a little disappointed in them. To see others throwing up warns you to think twice before helping someone who is trying to seek your assistance for a project he is trying to get off the ground. He is not being one hundred percent honest!

Warts say to the dreamer that he or she is looking at the world through distorted eyes. But there's no distorting the fact that dreams featuring warts say that someone is suggesting that your name and honour are not exactly synonymous and you may have quite a struggle to quell such talk. If you dream of having warts on your hands one minute and then seeing them vanish the next, than any obstacles you find on the path to good fortune will be easily cleared. And to see them afflicting others suggests that your enemies are gathering and plotting against you.

X-ray machines, like trusses, feature but rarely in dreams. But on the odd occasion that they do, they serve as a warning that someone in a position of some power is delving into the dreamer's life trying to uncover some secret, which if unearthed and made public could cause considerable distress to the dreamer. So if there is something in your past that you would prefer to stay there, make sure that your secret is safe, or remember the old adage that

A-Z OF DREAMS

• •

confession is good for the soul; it could also be good for your quality of life.

A Pavilion of Dreams

Despite our reputation for turning into a generation of couch potatoes, we are still remarkably sporting nations, which is probably why sports and related matters feature so much in dreams.

Baseball, when seen in the field of dreams, tells the dreamer that if he put his mind to it he could achieve much more than he already has. But if he is happy with things as they are, why pitch for more? For young women to dream that they are playing baseball suggests that their lives are too full of pleasures of a short-lasting kind.

Billiards warns that there is a lawsuit on the cards, probably one concerning property, and that the other party or parties involved might resort to slander to increase their chances of victory.

Bowling may well be the peaceful pastime of many of our senior citizens, but when a dreamer rolls a bowl through the dreamland green he should take it as a warning that he is participating in something, maybe a secret affair, that will not only bring shame, but could also cost him friends and money.

Boxing seen from the spectators' point of view warns that events may be about to swing out of control in many aspects of the dreamer's life and it's time to change one's ways. For a man to see himself in the ring is a sign that he knows that a confrontation that he has long been putting off cannot be put off for much longer. For a woman to see herself squaring up to an opponent in the ring is a sign that her friends are worried that her forward behaviour is making her the centre of gossip.

Diving, if the water is clear, tells the dreamer that any embarrassment that has been rippling around him will soon be a thing of the past. Making a splash in muddied waters, however, signifies that the dreamer is increasingly aware that life in general and business in particular may be about to take a turn for the worse. To see others enjoying diving says that the dreamer will be surrounded by good companions. And for lovers to dream that they are diving together tells them that they can look forward to a long life together and that the flames of passion will never cool.

Fencing is not such a common dream these days, but old times were full of dreams about fencing cavalier-like against an adversary. To sum up all the interpretations in a few apposite words for the third millennium, to see oneself with foil, sabre or épée in hand is an indication that the dreamer is ambitious to raise his social standing to new levels. But what you want and what you get may not be same thing!

Fishing casts good and bad news across the landscape of dreams. To see yourself hooking a fish is a sign of calm waters and good times ahead. But if nothing takes the bait, then remember that, in the words of Robert Burns, 'The best-laid schemes o' mice an' men gang aft agley'! But there's a good side to an empty fishing basket after a long time with the rod: that shows patience and determination that will eventually result in solid achievement.

Football is a difficult dream to interpret as despite its long history, its surge in popularity has been comparatively recent. Most current dream interpreters consider that to dream of football is to suggest that the dreamer is living with his head in the clouds when, if he is to do anything with his life, he should make sure his feet are planted firmly on the ground.

A-Z OF DREAMS

Golf is a signal to the dreamer that he is wishing his life away.

Gymnastics suggest that the dreamer is over ambitious and that in the competition to take the gold medal for life-achievement he will be lucky if he makes it past the qualifying heats!

Horseracing features occasionally in dreams and when it does the colour of the horse is considered more important than the actual activity. If the dreamer sees himself astride a white horse, then not just good, but tremendously good news is in the offing. The word often associated with that perfectly nice colour, bay, is, 'nice'. Nice things will happen – nothing special, but nice just the same! At best, a man who sees himself atop a bay mare may have a nice relationship with a nice woman (and the affair will certainly have its moments) but the flames of passion will soon die. To be seen riding a black horse is an indication, for a woman, that her husband or partner is being unfaithful. On a subject related to horseracing, jockeys suggest that a surprise windfall is on the cards.

Hunting for foxes is now banned in some parts of the world but enthusiastically pursued in others, and suggests that no matter how hard you try, what you really want out of life, whether in matters material or spiritual, will never be achieved. If the dream concerns game hunting, on the other hand, obstacles put in your path can be successfully cleared and your goals reached. If the dream concerns hounds rather than horses, and the dreamer is a woman, then she will marry beneath her. If they feature in a male dream, then the dreamer may marry a woman of ill repute. As someone said, perhaps they should meet.

Ice-skating warns of a loss of some sort, maybe something the dreamer treasures, but more likely to be loss of a job. If the ice breaks, then the dreamer is being warned to look outside his usual circle of friends for advice, for those to whom he usually looks for counsel could well let him down. If just the skates are seen on their own, then the dreamer should be warned that petty squabbles, particularly among business acquaintances, could be about to muddy the waters.

Javelins say that the dreamer's reputation is about to be pierced in some way that will result in his dirty laundry being washed in public before his reputation for honesty and fidelity is restored. To see someone carrying a javelin, means that the dreamer's interests are under threat. To see oneself

• •

pierced by a javelin means that someone is out to get you, and will succeed.

Mountaineering not unnaturally suggests that ambitions are yet to be realized and that the closer the dreamer sees himself to the top, then the closer to achieving his ambitions he is. Often the dreamer sees himself as being almost there but realizes that the last step is the most difficult to take. But hold on. The summit is there to be scaled. And if he has reached the peak, then that's it. At best, the dreamer is on a plateau as far as career matters are concerned: at worst, it's downhill from now onwards!

Racquets – tennis, badminton or squash – denote that just when the dreamer thinks he has something he has long wished for within his grasp it will be snatched away from him. For a young woman to have this dream is indicative of the fact that something will happen to prevent her taking part in an event she has been eagerly looking forward to.

Riding (see **Hunting**).

Shooting game is a pointer to the fact that the dreamer may be motivated by selfishness but he will probably get what he aims for. If the game comes within range but manages to evade capture or death, then the dreamer had better start paying attention to business matters or else a considerable loss may be experienced.

Sprinting in a race suggests that others share your ambitions and that whoever puts his mind to it will be first to break the winning tape. And it could be you!

Swimming easily through calm water tells the dreamer that something that has been worrying him will soon be left well behind. If, however, the strokes are laboured, then things may start to get a bit rough. To see oneself swimming underwater is a sign that anxious times are coming into the dreamer's ken.

A Theatre of Dreams

Dreams concerning entertainments being enjoyed either actively or passively are usually to be welcomed in the dreamscape for they presage good things in store – although there are exceptions, of course. Interpreting dreams about the theatre depends on which part of the theatre features, but generally because the theatre is a social venue it has relevance to our relationships with other people. Dreams that feature musical instruments can sometimes suggest attitudes to the dreamer's sexuality. They can also be symbolic of communication skills and abilities.

Accordion music says that the dreamer may be sad or introspective now but that something good is about to happen which will not only cheer him up immediately but help him view the future more cheerfully. If a woman dreams that she is playing the accordion, then she will find lasting marital happiness through the misfortune of another woman. If the accordion suddenly goes out of tune, then her lover may be about to fall ill or face trouble of another sort that will cause her much sadness.

A-Z OF DREAMS

· ·

Acrobats tumbling their way through dreams presage several things. Generally, when seen they tell the dreamer that the fears of others concerning a new business venture should be listened to, for what is being proposed could turn out to be financially risky despite appearances. If it is a female who is the acrobat, business affairs could well be about to be adversely affected by malicious gossip. If it is the dreamer who is up to acrobatic tricks, he is being warned that the schemes of enemies are about to make life unendurable. If the dreamer sees himself having an accident during a bout of acrobatics, then he will have a lucky escape in business or personal life.

Actors strutting their stuff in dreams proclaim several meanings. To see an actress says that things are on the up and will stay that way for the immediate future. If the actress is obviously unhappy, then a friend who has been suffering in silence for some reason, will turn to the dreamer for help which will be gladly given. If the dreamer is treading the boards, then life may not ever be particularly easy, but neither will it be particularly hard. To dream of a dead actor is just about as bad for the dreamer as it is for the actor, as times of turbulent unhappiness lie ahead. For a woman to dream that she is married or engaged to an actor is to be told that love will soon lose its shine. For a man to have the same dream tells him that his current lover might not be the one to settle down with! If the dream involves becoming enamoured of a thespian type, then it's likely that the dreamer is more concerned with the good life than in applying himself to his actual profession.

Ballet has featured in dream research for over two centuries probably because so many ballets from around the beginning of the nineteenth century featured dream sequences. Dreaming of performing in a ballet is a warning that, when awake, the dreamer should be more physical.

Balls where the dancing is jolly and the laughter gay signify that if happiness is not already smiling on you, then it is on the horizon. But if the music is slow and the dancers elderly, then a death might be waiting in the wings for a loved one.

Bugles when heard tell the dreamer that he can look forward to a period of exceptional peace and harmony at home. And if it is the dreamer that is blowing the bugle, then business is about to boom, too.

Clarinets suggest that the dreamer is about to cast dignity to the wind and indulge in the sort of frivolity not normally associated with him. A broken clarinet warns

● ●

the dreamer that something he has done, or is about to do, will cause a friend to become angry.

Clowns tell the dreamer that a relationship that he or she was hoping would develop into something serious, will fail to blossom into romance. If the clown's mask slips aside to reveal a leering grimace, then an acquaintance has duplicity in his heart. If the face that is revealed is a sad one, then try as you may to make someone believe that you are being serious, your efforts will go unrewarded, or worse, unnoticed. And finally, to dream that you are a clown is a warning that you will do something that will cause peers to sneer at you for some reason, however well intentioned your behaviour.

Compact discs may be comparatively new arrivals on the dreamscape, but they have acquired the meaning that you will soon be involved in a new relationship and that it will proceed very smoothly.

Cymbals making themselves heard in dreams are bad news – very bad news, for they indicate that an old person both in terms of age and the length of friendship will soon die.

● ●

Dancing is a happy dream with a happy message. Married dreamers who see children tripping the light fantastic will be blessed with a happy home life and a large family. Younger people who dream of dancing can expect a smooth path through life for the immediate future. If you dream that you are being taught to dance, there will be a strong temptation to neglect business and pursue insignificant pleasures: do not give into them, for if you do, the outcome could be disastrous. Different sorts of dances have slightly different meanings, but as most of them signify pleasant activities and good companionship, they do not have to be looked at individually – unless the dreamer is a woman and she is waltzing with her lover, for she will change partners many times in her life but never find true happiness with any of them.

Discotheques say that a new relationship is about to be forged and that it will leave the dreamer feeling confused and unable to concentrate on matters in hand.

Fireworks when cascading through a woman's dream, presage travel to somewhere she has never been before and that the trip will be an exceptionally pleasant one. To dreamers of either sex, they indicate good health and a sunny time ahead. More specifically,

● ●

if the firework is a Roman candle then you will achieve what you want in the immediate future, but if the firework fizzles out, then so too will the ambition.

Flutes bring a pleasant note to dreamers of either sex. For a man, flute music suggests that old friends who have been off the social scene for some time are about to reappear, maybe flying in after a long absence abroad. The sweet sound of the flute also tells him that a business venture will bear more fruit than expected. A woman who dreams that she is playing the flute may be about to meet a man whose manners are so delightful that he will win her heart.

Guitars simply seen being played have dual meanings. It can mean that friends are about to flock around the dreamer and bring much merriment into his life. Or to dreamers who are unattached romantically, they can mean that Cupid's arrow is about to hit carrying everlasting love in its dart. But if the dreamer is a young woman and the guitar has broken strings then her love life is about to take a turn for the worse.

Horns heard herald good news already winging its way to the dreamer, but if the dream features a broken horn, then far from presaging good news, there is a serious accident, maybe a fatal one, waiting to happen!

If the dreamer is a woman whose affections are engaged and she sees herself blowing a horn, then her feelings are stronger than her lover's.

Jesters signify that the dreamer has his priorities all wrong and that if things are not to go totally askew, it's time to stop chasing the elusive butterfly of frivolity and turn attention to more serious matters.

Lutes, when the dreamer is playing one, herald that good news from a friend who has not been seen for some time is on its way. To dream of hearing lute music suggests that the immediate future will be filled with happy occupations.

Lyres, when being played by a female dreamer, are a sign that she will become the centre of attention of a worthy and noble man, while to dream of listening to lyre music suggests that business affairs will go smoothly, companions will be merry and that great pleasure will be attained by following innocent pursuits.

Music (also see individual instruments) can be good or bad. Heard being played tunefully it presages good times ahead. Heard being played badly suggests that misbehaved children will cause disruptions in the house.

A-Z OF DREAMS

Musical instruments generally herald that the outlook is good, unless they are broken, in which case, for men, anticipated pleasures will be marred by unexpected bad company. Strangely, for a woman to dream of broken instruments, tells her that her future is in her own hands and that if she works hard enough there is little that cannot be achieved.

Orchestras presage a happy love life and good times on the horizon if the dreamer is one of the players. If he hears the music of an unseen orchestra, then he will be the centre of a happy circle of friends.

Organs, being played at their thundering best, tell the dreamer that friendships now being forged will be long-lasting and that plans concerning future financial security will flourish. But to see an organ in a church or chapel is a warning that someone in the immediate family is about to leave for pastures new, or worse, may die. If it is the organist being dreamed about, the dreamer is being warned that the thoughtless actions of a friend will result in the dreamer's nose being put out of joint. If a woman sees herself sitting at an organ it portends that her lover will abandon her unless she becomes less demanding, emotionally and sexually.

A THEATRE OF DREAMS

• •

Pianos presage great joy ahead when they are seen but not heard. When dreamers hear lovely music being played on a piano they can look forward to a healthy, wealthy future. But if the music is tuneless and inharmonious then lots of little irritations are on their way. If the music is sad and wistful, then if sad news is not already on its way to you, it soon will be. To see a broken piano says that others may well hold the dreamer in regard but that he is not satisfied with what he has achieved. It also says that the dreamer's children will not do as well as had been hoped.

Plays are the thing, and the thing they mean in dreams depends on the type of play and the sex of the dreamer. If a woman dreams that she is watching a play she is being told that she will receive many proposals from attractive suitors and that her choice will eventually be made for financial rather than romantic reasons. If she is on her way to the theatre and there is a hold-up of some sort, then unpleasant surprises are about to occur. These are also presaged by a play that is particularly bloody. If the play is a drama, then old friends who have been away for some time, are about to reappear and the friendship will grow and become deeper than it used to be. If the drama is tedious and the dreamer is bored, then he may be about to be forced into the company of an unpleasant person. If the play is a comedy, then the immediate future is going to be filled with happiness. To be in the audience while a tragedy is being acted out foretells that great disappointments are about to cloud the sky and that a misunderstanding will make the sky even darker. And don't even ask what is about to befall you if you dream that you are in the cast rather than the audience, for 'troublous times' loom.

Quartets have two meanings. If the dreamer is one of the four making music, then good times are in the offing and friends old and new will be especially supportive. But if the dreamer is a mere spectator, then something aspired to will always be just beyond reach.

Radios broadcast good news to the dreamer. If he is listening to one, then a new friend will widen the dreamer's horizons and awaken him to all sorts of exciting possibilities. If the radio is on in the background, a windfall could be on the radio waves.

Roundabouts curiously signify that the dreamer is about to experience a period where nothing will go right and that business affairs may start to stagnate. If the dreamer is a spectator rather than one of the carousers, then hopes will go unfulfilled and dreams

• •

turn to dust. If the roundabout is standing alone with nothing else on the landscape, then a period of great unhappiness is about to descend on the dreamer.

Shakespeare with around 37 plays to his pen and quotes from many of them known to millions of us, has his own entry in the *dramatis personae* of dreams. To see the bard warns that unhappy times are in the offing, especially for those in love. For a young person to dream that he is reading Shakespeare is an indication that he has a deep love of literature and may well seek his career in publishing or a related occupation.

Singing says that good news is wafting or is about to waft its way towards the dreamer, unless the song is a doleful one, in which case then things might be about to take a turn for the worse. If it's a bass voice, then the dreamer would do well to keep an eye on business matters, for an employee could be taking advantage of a *laissez-faire* attitude. For those in love, a deep singing voice warns that tiffs and quarrels could be about to become more common. A duet says that bad news about an absent friend is about to be received, but that will bring a little light relief. Choir music presages that the cobwebs of gloom are about to be blown away, unless the dreamer is a woman, in which case her lover might be about to be tempted by the attractions of not just one but several other women.

Tambourines are not usually heard in dreams so it is appropriate that their meaning indicates an enjoyable event will happen in an unusual location.

Televisions, when being viewed by the dreamer, indicate that you are too easily swayed. This message is reinforced if what you are watching is making you feel uncomfortable. To see one's own face on television is a sign that your friends see you as vain and shallow as a puddle, and this may lead to your heart being broken.

Theatres are often seen during the sleeping hours. To dream of being in the audience foretells new friendships are about to be forged and that they will bring much happiness into the dreamer's life. But while, for members of the audience, things should run smoothly in the immediate future, a dreamer who sees himself in the cast should make the most of the good things in life for they may be about to evaporate. If the show is a variety one, then the pursuit of pleasure may start to cost the dreamer dear in business affairs. If a pantomime is in progress, then assumed friends might soon reveal themselves to be false. An opera on the other hand says that friends are about to add significantly to the quality of life and that things will go smoothly in career and business matters. Someone who sees himself applauding or laughing in the theatre, may be about to turn their back on duty and embrace fanciful pursuits. If for some reason the theatre has to be evacuated, the dreamer should think twice before getting involved with a business proposition.

Trumpets when seen but not heard foretell that something unusual but extremely interesting is about to happen. If the dreamer is blowing his trumpet then his good fairy is about to wave her wand and make his dreams come true.

Ventriloquists have an obvious meaning to dreamers and that is to be warned to take nothing at face value. If someone says something to you think twice before acting on their words, especially in business matters. For a dreamer to see himself as the voice behind the doll, then he is not acting properly towards people who trust him.

Violins say to the dreamer, 'Relax. You are the centre of a warm, loving family and our financial affairs are in perfect order.' If the violin is more fiddle than Stradivarius, that message is reinforced and as a

A-Z OF DREAMS

● ●

bonus, a trip overseas will soon create a happy diversion from humdrum, everyday living. When a young woman dreams that she is making sweet music on a violin she can expect an honour of some sort, accompanied by rich gifts. But if her music is out of tune, then she will soon find herself falling out of favour with her friends and the things to which she aspires will never be hers.

A Journey of Dreams

Just as we daydream in the dark days of winter about being transported to faraway places, so in our dreams we often dream of travelling and all that involves – cars and trucks, and planes and trains. Indeed, what are dreams if they are not part journeys themselves? Generally, to dream of travelling indicates that a pleasurable experience will lead to unexpected financial gain, while travelling on your own suggests that you may have to make a trip to settle some sort of problem that has been nagging you for ages.

If you see yourself travelling to a place you have never been to before, then two things may be indicated, neither of them nice: it could be that enemies are out to get you. And it could be that the enemy has no human form but will present itself in the form of sickness.

If you see yourself travelling over a barren, rocky landscape, then a business venture may turn out to be profitable, but the gains will be short-lived and will vanish almost as soon as they present themselves. But if you are travelling over fertile hills, then the

● ●

foundations from which the profit has been gained are deep and long-term wealth is indicated.

If the dreamer sees himself setting out on a long journey then sees himself arriving at his destination almost as soon as he has set out, he could be being given advance notice that a project he has set aside a fair bit of time to complete will be finished much more quickly than had been anticipated. And that at the end he will have an enhanced reputation and a healthier bank balance.

Aeroplanes have several meanings, the two most common of which are as follows. To see one vanish in the sky suggests that the dreamer is about to face an unpleasant situation of some sort but that nothing serious will happen to him. To be a passenger on a plane is a good sign, suggesting that plans being laid, especially speculative ones, will come to profitable fruition.

Buses have various meanings for the dreamer. Those who see themselves sitting in a passenger seat have a strong hint that career matters are grinding to a standstill. If the dreamer is standing in a crowded bus, then competition for the next step up the career ladder will be intense. And if you see yourself going in the wrong direction, then not only are you going the wrong way in your dreams, you are going in the wrong direction in career matters. Get off the road you are on; think about what you really want to do, not what others expect you to do and you'll be on the right track.

Canoes are good news – and bad. To see himself paddling a canoe across still waters is a sign that the dreamer is confident in his abilities to keep his business affairs in apple-pie order – perhaps overconfident, which could cause ripples to spread. On the romantic front, for a man to see himself paddling his girlfriend in a canoe is a sign that wedding invitations are about to be sent out, and that the marriage will be long and happy. But if the waters turn choppy, once wed, the bride could turn out to be something of a Xanthippe and she will, to use a term more usually applied to pet dogs, be brought to heel! If the canoe runs aground in shallow waters, a whirlwind romance will lead to a stormy marriage. If the waters turn muddy, then the dreamer could find himself in some murky business.

Driving a coach signifies that change is afoot in business matters. Business is also behind things when the dreamer sees himself as a passenger: in this case business losses are just around the corner.

A-Z OF DREAMS

Driving a taxi warns that the dreamer's career prospects are not so good and that they may never rise above working at the more menial jobs.

Helicopters hovering in the air above your head say that a friend is about to drop in unexpectedly. If the aircraft starts to wobble dangerously, there will be a visit but not from a friend.

Losing luggage (and who among us has not in real life stood by a baggage carousel at an airport, quite convinced that our luggage will never appear?) is a common dream. In dreams it denotes that a recent investment might prove to be unwise. It's not necessarily a financial investment: it could be that we invested time unwisely, or our emotions. The outcome could be distress in the family, particularly if it is the latter case. If a single person dreams of losing his or her luggage, then a broken engagement is foretold.

Luggage portends that the dreamer will soon be weighed down with burdensome and unpleasant duties, probably involving people whom the dreamer finds unsavoury. To see oneself carrying one's own luggage while porters are standing around doing nothing suggests that something so distressing is about to happen that will preoccupy the dreamer to such an extent that he will be blind to the concerns of others.

Plane crashes are not quite as bad in dreams as they are in real life. They don't necessarily mean death is about to be dealt to the dreamer, but they do suggest that plans will go awry and that there could be bad news about a relation winging its way towards you!

Porters when simply seen suggest that you will soon be weighed down with bad luck. For dreamers to see themselves as porters says that they are lacking in ambition and that they should pull their socks up. To dream that one is hiring a porter suggests that the dreamer will enjoy some success. And to see oneself paying a porter for his services is a warning that you will stand accused of a criminal charge, more irritating than serious – a parking ticket, perhaps, or a speeding offence.

Railway track suggests that the dreamer would do well to keep close track of business affairs as someone he trusts is plotting against him. If the dreamer is a woman, a visit to some friends who she has not seen for some time is heralded.

Riding bicycles is a good omen for men, not so good for women. For a man, pedalling uphill tells him that his prospects are getting brighter the harder he pedals. For a woman, however, to see herself riding downhill warns her that her good name may be about to be called into question and her health might be on the wane.

Riding motorcycles tells the rider that he is firmly in the driving seat as far as personal relationships are concerned. To see someone else astride a bike is a warning that while all around you are doing well, you are at a standstill in your career and lovelife.

Rowing boats can be difficult to control and if someone dreams that the boat he is rowing overturns, he should beware of being asked to participate in a new business: more than likely it will go belly-up like the boat. But if the boat gets to its destination safely, the dreamer is set to enjoy the company of sophisticated and fun people.

Ships are welcome in the logbook of dreams for generally they indicate that the dreamer will rise far above the station to which he was born. Ships sailing through stormy waters warn that business is about to take a downturn, probably because of the deliberate actions of a colleague or employee. And if the dreamer hears word of a shipwreck, then the perfidious person will, in all likelihood be a woman! To lose one's life in a shipwreck warns that the dreamer will sail close to the

● ●

wind and might be about to have a near-death experience. And to see others perish in a shipwreck indicates that a friend will turn to you to save him from the disgrace of bankruptcy.

Taxis have two meanings. If the journey is during daylight hours, then the dreamer's career prospects are no better and no worse than anyone else's. If it's dark outside, then you will be party to a secret that must be kept from everyone – at any cost.

The underground signifies a bumpy ride ahead, probably on the emotional front. And if the train grinds to a halt between stations then the dreamer will soon find himself on the horns of a moral dilemma of some sort.

Trains that are progressing smoothly along a railless track suggest that worries over a business opportunity recently grasped will prove unfounded and that money will soon start to flow in. But to see a freight train says that your career is on track and that you could be in for an unexpected promotion. If you see yourself settling down for the night in a sleeper then beware for you are fast acquiring the reputation for being someone who is unscrupulous in the pursuit of wealth. If a dream train is travelling at breakneck speed, foreign travel is forecast, perhaps related to a promotion at work. If it breaks down, don't depend on business affairs going well: they probably won't. A train heard approaching says that news from abroad is whistling down the line towards you, again probably to do with work.

Tramcars may be good news for city commuters, but they presage bad things for dreamers. To see one is to be warned that someone is out to get you and is whispering vicious slanders behind your back. To see yourself riding on a tramcar warns that your personal happiness is under threat from a jealous rival. And for a man to dream that he is standing on the platform waiting to get off says that his fancy is about to wander and that when his partner finds out, he'd better watch out, for hell hath no fury like a woman scorned!

Trunks, foretell that Lady Luck has turned her back on the dreamer, unless he or she is packing the trunk, in which case an enjoyable journey is on the horizon. If what was in the trunk is now scattered in disarray around a room, a journey will have to be planned at extremely short notice, maybe as the result of a quarrel, and the outcome will be far from satisfactory. An empty trunk warns that the search for romantic attachment will end in disappointment.

A Model of Dreams

Some of the dream themes mentioned here occur elsewhere in relevant sections in this book. Flying, for instance, appears in the chapter on transport. We repeat them here because they are often regarded as 'typical dreams' – dreams that are universal, seen by all races and regarded by psychologists, dream interpreters and seers to be alike in the frequency with which they appear and the similarity of their content. The reason for many of these dreams often has a physical cause as well as an underlying psychological significance.

Balancing on the edge of a cliff is thought to point to some unconscious fear that the dreamer is refusing to acknowledge. Or it may be either that a particularly difficult task lies ahead that is causing the dreamer considerable concern or that a difficult choice has to be made, and the dreamer has no idea which option to go for. On the other hand, it has been suggested that the most likely reason for such a dream is that the sleeper has tossed and turned to such an extent that their feet are hanging over the edge of the bed!

A-Z OF DREAMS

Traditionally, the dream was thought to be a warning of some sort.

Being burgled may suggest that everyday noises have crept into the sleeper's consciousness but are not sufficiently loud to waken him or her. Freud believed the dream was caused by a fear that emotional and sexual privacy was being invaded in some way. Dream interpreters of earlier times said that if the dreamer saw himself challenging a burglar and sending him on his way it meant that a victory over enemies was within view, while to be beaten back by a burglar indicated that it was the dreamer's enemies who would emerge victorious.

Climbing a hill may be a manifestation of a heart or lung condition that has still to be diagnosed by a doctor. Raphael and other more mystical interpreters believe that this dream along with those where the dreamer's physical effort is drawing sweat says that the dreamer has an ambitious nature. If there are obstacles that have to be overcome, then there is likely to be an obstacle in the dreamer's realization of the ambition.

Death, be it of a parent or dead people in general, is
commonly held to reflect a feeling of sorrow and an
unease that trouble may be brewing. Freud took the
view that the meaning of the typical Death Dream
depends on the reaction of the dreamer to the death.
If he or she is unmoved then the dream should not be
considered typical. Rather, it symbolizes a wish that the
dreamer wants something to end, not someone to die.
Attendant grief brings the dream into the 'typical'
category where it signifies that the dreamer wants, or
at some time in the past, wanted the person seen as
dead in the dream out of their lives – forever! Romany
folk believe that to dream of death indicates the
possibility of a birth or a change of circumstances
either in the dreamer's life or in the lives of those in his
or her family circle. Other interpretations include
disappointments and sorrow looming ahead, especially
if the dream concerns seeing members of one's
immediate family as being dead. The deaths of less
close family members or friends warn that the persons
concerned could soon approach the dreamer with
some very depressing news (not necessarily of a fatal
nature). To dream of dying warns of a threat of evil
emanating from a previously friendly source: perhaps
someone thought to be a friend is about to reveal
themselves in their true colours. To see someone the
dreamer doesn't recognize shuffle off their mortal coil

● ●

says that bad luck is about to make itself felt. If the dream concerns an imminent death rather than actually passing over to the other side, again ill luck is presaged if not to the dreamer then to someone in his or her immediate circle.

Exams were once thought to feature only in the dreams of people who have passed them, never by those of us who failed one or two during our educational careers! But this theory is no longer given credence. The dream of sitting an exam and being completely unprepared for it is not exclusive to students. It is a typical dream that can occur at any time at any age once the dreamer has had experience of being in an exam situation (which nowadays seems to happen at an ever-earlier age!) The dream probably reflects that dreamer's feeling of being under pressure at work or in a relationship.

Falling is very similar in origin to the typical Flying Dream, (see below) but there are some differences in its interpretation. Most straightforwardly, the dream may be caused by the fact that as someone drifts off into sleep they may lose awareness that they are in bed and feel unsupported, hence they dream of falling! Havelock Ellis, a nineteenth/twentieth-century physician who wrote widely about sex, thought that when the typical falling dream recurs at the end of a flying dream, it might suggest that the dreamer is of an especially nervous disposition. Freud, typically, put the dream down to eroticism, believing it to be a sexual dream of fear, but added that in women it may have its origin in a deep-rooted fear of being seen as immoral. Gypsies believe that the dream forewarns of loss and of being crossed in love, but claim that if the dreamer falls then picks himself up, a change of some sort, maybe a move to a new area, is on the cards. And Raphael, a nineteenth-century astrologer who claimed that his Royal Book of Dreams was based on an ancient manuscript he unearthed, writes that the dreamer who dreams of falling will lose a sweetheart or, to sailors, it can warn of shipwreck.

Flying (which includes **gliding**, **hovering**, and **rising**) takes its symbolism from the legend of Icarus, who, when escaping from Crete with his father, Daedalus, flew too close to the sun. As a result, the wax holding his wings together melted and he crashed to his death in the sea thousands of feet below. St Jerome, who made the first translation of the Bible from Hebrew into Latin, attributed dreaming of flying to God's grace, and there are many Christians and theosophists today who interpret the dreams corroborating the spirit's desire to break free from the body corporeal.

A-Z OF DREAMS

• •

Romany folk believe that flying is a fortunate thing to dream of. Raphael, on the other hand says, 'To dream of flying denotes that you will escape many difficulties and angers. If you dream that you are trying to fly very high, you will aspire to a position you will never reach and for which you are not qualified.' He goes on to say that to servants, the dream means a desire for liberty and to the poor it means a wish for wealth. Wingless flight high above the ground, means some sort of fear and danger while to fly low over the rooftops heralds trouble and rebellion of some sort.

Havelock Ellis believed flying to be the most widely experienced and oldest typical dream. He traced it back to the time when people started to become aware of the spiritual side of life and turned their minds heavenwards. He believed dream flying to be the result of the rhythm of the rise and fall of the sleeper's respiratory organs. He also pointed out that people who dream that they come back, unconscious, from the very brink of death, reported that they had experienced a feeling of flying, as though their souls were striving to reach heavenward.

Freud, as one would expect, put the typical flying dream down to sex and interpreted it according to the dreamer's age, experience, level of sexual activity and their sexuality, acknowledged or not! But basically he believed that the dream has its origin in the childhood desire to shake off the shackles of convention and restraint, which is why the dream is invariably accompanied by a delightful sense of freedom.

Missing a train was considered by Freud to indicate a fear of death, a feeling of sexual inadequacy or of being incapable of coping with some relationship or other. Havelock Ellis takes a much more prosaic view. According to his writing, missing a train indicated that the dreamer had a headache! Others agree – almost, believing as they do that the underlying cause is physical or mental exhaustion. Some interpreters see the dream as suggesting a regret of missed opportunities or an acknowledgement that the dreamer is unable to cope with life as it is now. A more imaginative interpretation is that missing a train indicates that a move of house or a long journey is likely or that a friend from far away is about to visit.

Nudity and being scantily dressed, by consensus, occurs in dreams when the sleeper has thrown off the covers and is consequently feeling exposed. But Freud, as he is wont to, brings sex into the frame writing that to dream of being indifferent to being seen naked or wearing clothes that leave nothing to the

● ●

imagination reflects the dreamer's desire to abandon restraint. But if he or she is desperately ashamed of the naked state, sexual guilt is the cause. Less informed opinion holds that the Naked Dream predicts disgrace or embarrassment, and to the Romany it heralds a period of poverty, ill health and all-round bad luck.

School days in dreams are thought to be caused by the sleeping body being cramped, which brings to the dreamer's mind how he or she had to squeeze themselves into their school desks, especially when they were older. The dream is considered by most interpreters to indicate that the dreamer lacks confidence either in the workplace or in their day-to-day relationships within the family.

Swimming, according to Freud, has associations with childhood eroticism. Havelock Ellis associated it with the respiratory process and added that the dream is sometimes associated with the skin being stimulated in some way. Raphael put his own, vaguely supernatural interpretation on the swimming dream, claiming that seeing oneself with head held high above the water signifies business success and enjoyable love affairs. If the head was underwater, however, a dream dip heralds unpleasant news and trouble in the offing. He has more to say on the subject, writing that if the water is dirty, the swimmer is about to be unjustly slandered. And if he starts to sink, then gloom, doom and ruination will flood the dreamer's life.

Teeth falling out usually feature in dreams when the dreamer is a tooth-grinder or has some sort of dental irritation. Freud opined that such a dream signifies that the dreamer sees himself as being sexually immature or insecure. Raphael believed that a loose tooth warned of oncoming illness, while losing one tooth or more was a sign that a death was imminent! Other oneiromancers [dream interpreters] concur to a certain extent with him on this, writing that the dream suggests that sorrow is in the air.

A Forecast of Dreams

The weather is one of the controlling factors in all our lives. Not surprisingly therefore weather features quite commonly in our dreams.

Clear skies tell the dreamer that he is generally well-liked by everyone who knows him, and that if there are any enemies they will soon make their peace. If something has been lost, it will be found and if there is a lawsuit in the offing, victory will be the dreamer's.

Clouds, if they are dark and threatening, suggest that misfortune of some serious kind is blowing in. Light, wispy clouds foretell that something mysterious is about to occur: not necessarily unpleasant but something that will give the dreamer something to puzzle about.

Fog warns the dreamer that before he can fully understand a problem he is facing, he will have to look at it much more closely than he has done.

Gales warn that business losses are about to disrupt the dreamer's life. To a blue-collar worker they

● ●

suggest trouble in the workplace, cut-backs perhaps leading to redundancy.

Hail when heard drumming on the roof is a warning that something distressing is about to hit. If the dreamer sees himself being caught in a hailstorm, then success will always be within reach, but never actually grasped. But if the sun breaks through before the hail goes off, then that success will come to hand. For a woman to dream this tells her that after many disappointments true love will be hers.

Ice suggests that his or her partner is seeing the dreamer as increasingly cold, physically and emotionally. It can also point to a loss of libido, in male dreams. To see ice floating on water, warns that ill-natured and envious friends will cause you unhappiness. Eating ice is a warning of on-coming ill health, while drinking ice water is a signal to eat and drink less: if the warning goes unheeded then illness is more or less guaranteed. If a dreamer sees himself diving into icy water, then an expected happening will mar an outing that is being anticipated with some happiness. Perhaps the simplest interpretation of an icy dream is that the sleeper has kicked the duvet from the bed and is freezing!

● ●

Icicles in a young woman's dream predict that marriage is on the cards and that the man proposing marriage will be older than the dreamer, and wealthier. If the icicles are falling from trees, a current difficulty will soon disappear. Hanging from trees they signify ill health waiting in the wings. If they are hanging from the eaves of houses things may start to get a bit tight.

Lightning that strikes an object close to the dreamer causing them to feel the shock is a warning that your name is on the tongues of malicious gossip-mongers. It also means that good fortune about to hit a friend will have an adverse affect on the dreamer. To be struck by lightning means that something terrible is about to happen in business or love affairs. But if the lightning flashes above the dreamer's head, happiness and a windfall of some sort are coming the dreamer's way.

Rain has several meanings. Torrential rain points to feelings of depression. Heavy rain suggests that the dreamer wants to be cleansed of something that has stained his past. Light rain suggests that the dreamer's life is about to change in some way. To dream of a deluge means that financial ruin is about to stare the dreamer in the face.

Snow is said to mean that prosperity is about to enrich the dreamer's life. If he is already prosperous, then he will become even more so. That is the interpretation put on snow by Romany folk: other dream interpreters say that to dream of snow is a warning that while there will be no real misfortunes in the dreamer's path through life, there might be bouts of ill health that could affect career prospects. To dream of eating snow is indicative that ideals will never be realized. If the snow is grey and dirty it warns that pride goes before a fall and that the fall is just around the corner. Such snow can also mean that someone you have been holding in contempt will do something to redeem themselves in your opinion and that you will take the necessary steps to bring about reconciliation. A dream that you are looking through a window at a fall of large, white snowflakes warns that financial depression will cause rows with your sweetheart. If you dream that you are snowbound, wave after wave of bad luck is about to crash down on you. And a final word on the meaning of snow in dreams – to see the sun shining on a snow-covered landscape says that the dreamer may be facing financial difficulties at present but that the sun will shine on his endeavours to overcome them and that he will prosper.

Thunder predicts business reversals while to be caught in a thunder storm warns that grief is about to wrap its arms around the dreamer!

A Miscellany of Dreams

If what you have dreamed about doesn't appear in the more specific sections of the book, you should find it here.

Abandoning (also see **Abandonment**, below) something bad in a dream is often a sign that you could quite possibly be about to receive news of a financial windfall. Another interpretation is that a trickle of bad news will become a flood and unhappiness will become so intense that the dreamer can see no way of ever getting back on an even keel. If a dreamer sees himself as abandoning his home, then he should resist any temptation to speculate financially for to do so will end in disaster and ruin. For a man to dream that he is abandoning his sweetheart heralds good news and bad. First the bad news: friends will desert the dreamer as quickly as rats flee the proverbial sinking ship. And the good news? Something of value that was lost and given up as gone forever will turn up unexpectedly. There's good news, too, if the dream concerns abandoning a mistress: news of an unexpected inheritance will soon be received. If the dream concerns abandoning children, an uncharacteristic lack of judgement will cause a downturn in fortune. To see oneself as abandoning a business in a dream is to be warned that the air will be clouded with arguments and quarrels that will leave businessmen worse off than they were. To dream of abandoning a ship can be bad or good. Bad in that it suggests that you will be involved in a business failure. Good in that if you make it safely to land, your losses will be minimal. And for a last word on abandoning, if the dream concerns abandoning his or her religion, then unwise words about people who have you in your power – your boss perhaps, or an important client – will cost you dear.

Abandonment, that dreadful feeling that someone you trusted has left you totally on your own, drifting around in an unknown landscape, is often a reflection that when you were a child, you were constantly afraid that you were unwanted by others in the family. Ninety-nine times out of one hundred this is compietely untrue, but the fear lingers on into adulthood and surfaces in the dreamer's mind as abandonment. When it appears regularly, the dreamer is often the type of person who has difficulty laying down plans to safeguard the future. It can mean trouble ahead, but if the dreamer takes it as a warning, then the trouble can usually be averted.

• •

Abduction may not be one of the most common of dreams, but when it does snatch the dreamer's attention, it is likely that he has been facing some sort of opposition, maybe in business or perhaps socially. The dream is a sign that this will be overcome and the desired success is waiting to be embraced. And if the dreamer witnesses someone being abducted, then some unexpected good news is imminent.

Abhorrence, when it is the dominant emotion in a dream, is a warning that danger and difficult times lie ahead. Usually they will present themselves from out of the blue and their influence on the dreamer's life depends on the degree of the emotion that is aroused. If it is intensely felt, then the potential to do harm is great: but if it is more strong annoyance than true abhorrence, then the difficulties will be easily overcome. Romanies believed that when the dreamer experienced abhorring someone, they would often be strongly suspicious of a person's behaviour and that these suspicions would prove to be well founded. If, on the other hand, it is the dreamer who sees himself as being held in abhorrence, then presently held good intentions to act for the general benefit in some scheme or other will slowly fade away to be replaced by selfish motives coming to the fore. And if the dreamer is a young woman whose affections are unengaged and she sees herself being abhorred by a lover, then she will fall in love. Sadly, the man with whom she eventually gives her heart will prove to be someone she will come to dislike intensely but from whom she will be unable to part.

Abortion is often seen as a need to reject an emotion or a belief, which the dreamer subconsciously sees as being a source of potential trouble. Maybe a risk has been taken which is not working out as was envisaged and the dream is an expression of a wish to turn the clock back. Abortion can also indicate that the dreamer is becoming aware that the time is right to give his life a good spring cleaning, discarding what is redundant to make way for new challenges and experiences. For the female dreamer, it is often seen as a sign that her health is on the decline.

Abroad, whether it be in a country the dreamer recognizes or an unfamiliar one, is an indication of a deeply felt need for personal freedom. Being abroad in a dream may indicate a desire to escape from a physical location or perhaps from a relationship or situation. To gypsies, it had two very straightforward meanings. Either that the dreamer was about to go travelling (very likely if the dreamer was also a gypsy) in the company of good friends, or that it may be necessary to leave one's present whereabouts and go and live abroad. Again quite likely given the gypsies' well-known dislike of being in one place for any great length of time. Another interpretation is that if the dreamer sees him or herself as travelling abroad by sea, then he or she may be about to make friends with people of considerable influence in the near future.

Absconding's meaning in the dream almanac depends on the sex of the dreamer. For men to either see themselves absconding or others doing so is an indication that colleagues at work may have smiles on their faces when they look at the dreamer, but scowls and sneers when he is out of view! And to the female dreamer, a similar dream should be taken as a warning to be extremely careful when deciding on whom to bestow affection.

Absence, either someone not being where they should be, or the absence of something that could be reasonably expected to be where it is not, can be taken as an indication that the unexpected is about to strike. And as it's unexpected, the dreamer is given no indication of when or where it will come from, or what form it will take! On a deep, psychological level, a dream of absence can be a spillover from the emotions felt when the child noticed for the first time that a parent (usually the mother) was not there. On a less serious note, if you dream that you are happy about the absence of a friend, then an enemy could be about to leave the scene. Whereas to dream of a sense of deep loss at the absence of someone suggests that at some time in the past the dreamer acted hastily and unwisely in doing something that is now deeply regretted. And in repenting for the deed, the foundations of a life-lasting friendship will be laid.

Abundance means the opposite in dreams of what it means in life – for if you dream that there is a great abundance of something it is a clear warning to conserve resources and energies for they could be about to be drained. A more traditional interpretation was that if a dreamer saw himself abundantly provided for Fortune would not so much smile on the dreamer's material life, she would positively grin at him. But it is a different matter on the domestic front, as riches come in one door, happiness slips out the window as his or her partner seeks comfort in someone else's arms.

Abuse's meaning depends on whether the dreamer is the abuser or the abused. If it is the former, then if you have acted in any way dishonourably towards friends, then the repercussions will start to be felt. Such antisocial behaviour can also mean that financial losses are on the cards because of an obstinate refusal to see that good money is being thrown after bad. If the dreamer is being abused, either physically, verbally or emotionally there is a strong likelihood that enemies will gain the upper hand, unless the dreamer takes what he sees as a warning to be on his guard.

Abusive language when heard in a woman's dream suggests that she will become the focus of another's jealousy and envy. If it is she who is doing the swearing society is about to turn its collective back on her because the unkindness she displayed towards friends in the past is about to become public knowledge.

An **abyss** is a reflection of the dreamer's recognition that at some time in life we all must come face to face with the unknown, which, when we face it, will cause us to take risks we have never even contemplated before. It can also suggest the dreamer's fear of losing control, or of a loss of identity or being seen as a failure. This may act as the spur to lead him or her on to exceed the self-imposed boundaries and become a stronger, more complete person. If there is a danger of falling into the abyss then a problem that is being currently faced will be seen off. But to stagger and fall into it, is to warn the dreamer that if he or she is to

● ◆

avoid a business loss they will have to be extremely careful. Romany folk believed that a dream in which an abyss features is a warning that someone has their eyes on your property and may be willing to resort to law to get their hands on it. Such a chasm may also portend that personal life in the immediate future will be marked by arguments that will be particularly vicious.

Accidents happen to all of us and feature widely in dreams. Such dreams serve as a warning to steer clear of whatever was involved in the dream accident no matter what. Many dreamers claim that heeding such warnings has saved their lives. For example, one dreamer who saw himself being in a car accident took to taking the bus to work. A few days later he passed an extremely bad crash at the exact spot he would have been and at the exact time he would have been there had he driven to work. If the dreamer sees himself as being badly injured, he should take it as a warning to beware the hidden aggression of others. Accidents can also highlight anxieties about safety and fears about taking on responsibilities. If the accident happens to an animal, then according to gypsy tradition, the dreamer will have to struggle with all his might to achieve what it is he wants and in attaining it, a friend or colleague will suffer a corresponding loss. If a public convenience is the cause of the accident, then the dreamer may well be about to suffer a loss or is in danger of being struck down by illness. If the dreamer is a young woman and she sees herself involved in a particularly bad accident, then her lover may well be planning to desert her without warning.

Acid signifies an awareness that there is something corrosive in the dreamer's life, which may be the cause of some unhappiness but which could be turned to the dreamer's advantage. It can also suggest that the dreamer feels that his self confidence is being eroded by circumstances beyond his control. The first step to getting it back is to recognize what is happening. A woman seeing herself drinking acid in her dreams denotes that she is about to be compromised and that as a result her health may be endangered. And for dreamers of either sex to see bottles of acid neatly stacked on a shelf is a warning that the stench of treachery is in the air.

Adultery, an increasingly common fact of modern life if divorce statistics are a reliable indicator of sexual as well as social mores, suggests that the dreamer is trying, or realizes he ought to try, to come to terms with his sexual needs and desires for stimulation and excitement. Dreaming of having an affair is the dreamer's way of releasing these feelings. Affairs may also be the psyche's way of seeking emotional satisfaction in our dreams in ways that are taboo when we are awake. If the dreamer sees his or her spouse as having an affair, this could be an expression of feelings of sexual inadequacy. Dream interpreters of days gone by held that the dreamer who saw himself committing adultery was prescient that some previously unknown criminal misdemeanour was about to be revealed and that the long arm of the law was about to tap the dreamer on the shoulder. If the dreamer was a female, her dream adultery was a warning to control her temper lest spiteful outbursts drive her husband to another's arms. And if she recognizes her illicit dream lover as being a friend of her husband's her husband will for no reason she can see pay less and less attention to her. Finally, if she sees herself as trying to entice a much younger man into her bed, her husband may be about to leave her and start divorce proceedings.

Advice given and advice received have their own meanings. To receive it in a dream tells us that we should listen to our 'inner voices' more than we do and that we should act on our instincts more than we do at present. It can also be an indication that we have been asked to do something and have agreed to it, despite the fact that we don't really want to. To dream of giving advice displays a willingness to share what we have – be it physical, spiritual or emotional – with others.

Affairs suggest that the dreamer needs to come to terms with his sexual needs and desires if he is to be a really rounded person. Seeing himself enjoying illicit company is also a sign that it is not just sex that should be attended to. Perhaps the dreamer is aware that other aspects of his life are out of balance and need attention.

Afternoons may not feature very often in dreams, but if they are what a female remembers as being the dominant theme, then she can look forward to new friendships – not superficial, social acquaintances, but deep friendships that will be enjoyed by all parties for the rest of their lives.

AIDS, a late twentieth-century fact of life is a very recent addition to the dream journal, and is seen as an expression of a deep-rooted fear of being permanently scarred in life. This may not be concerned with health – it could be that a bad career choice has ruined life. To dream that someone else has AIDS is indicative of a feeling of helplessness regarding some situation in which the dreamer is involved.

A-Z OF DREAMS

● ●

Aliens are significant that something frightening but
unknown may have to be faced in the near future. But
they can also suggest that the dreamer is aware that
he or she is different in some way from others and is
slowly realizing that this is nothing to worry about: we
are all different in our own ways and life is richer for it.
On the other hand, to dream that you are an alien
could be a warning that an interest in the occult is
taking too strong a hold. If the dream concerns being
abducted by aliens, this may be an expression of a fear
of change, especially in domestic affairs. Gypsies
believed that when aliens appeared in dreams, their
presence meant that the dreamer would meet people
whom he considered to be peculiar and in whose
company the dreamer would, at first, feel
uncomfortable. But the more they can get to know
each other, the more the dreamer can relax in their
company and the more influential they will become.

Anger is a commonly experienced emotion and is
often felt in dreams where it is seen as representing
the struggle to express ourselves properly. Anger,
when it dominates a dream can also be interpreted as
the mind's way of telling the dreamer that it is quite in
order for him or her to feel passionately about
something – and to give verbal expression to that
passion. If the anger is focused on someone the

dreamer knows, then the obvious interpretation is that that person has offended the dreamer and the dream is an expression of pent-up hostility. This, again, may be the result of being unable to express the anger in real life, for fear of causing offence. If the anger is being directed at the dreamer, then this is most likely a guilt thing: the dreamer is aware that he is responsible for something unsavoury and has not yet said, 'Sorry!' although he knows an apology is due. Traditional folklore held that when anger makes its presence felt, some terrible trial awaits the dreamer. It could concern being let down badly by a loved one, or that the ties that bind a long-valued friendship are about to be cut. It could even be that enemies who have been plotting the dreamer's downfall are about to see their plans come to successful fruition. If the dream concerns friends or family being angry with the dreamer, then he or she may be about to be called upon to mediate in some dispute – and will do so to the satisfaction of all concerned. According to one nineteenth-century sage, anger denotes that enemies (whose plots will threaten the dreamer's security and happiness) surround the dreamer, and that a rival for a lover's hand is whispering slander in his or her ear. A contemporary interpretation suggests that to dream of being angry with one's spouse was a signal that a period of unusual peace and harmony lay ahead on the domestic front. A less fanciful meaning is that anger in a dream is representative of other passionate emotions and that the dreamer is struggling to find the right way to express them.

Appetites do not commonly feature in dreams, but, according to one sage of days gone by, when someone wakes up and recalls that he or she has appeased the appetite by eating something of which they are particularly fond, then ill health is about to afflict the dreamer with a noticeable effect on the dreamer's appearance. He goes on to write that to be conscious of being hungry in a dream, is a sign that good friends are about to leave the scene, and that a falling appetite heralds bad news. Modern, more scientific interpreters suggest that such dreams represent an unfulfilled desire either physical or spiritual. Appetite is also thought to be indicative of an especially lusty nature.

Appointments suggest that the dreamer is aware that his or her life is lacking goals and that now is the time to start aiming for success. But if the dreamer misses an appointment, then this is indicative of an awareness that not enough attention is being paid to the details of life. Appointments can also suggest that the dreamer feels that he is due a reward for something that has been done and is feeling resentful that such reward has not been forthcoming.

Aprons can represent family ties or perhaps a badge of office. But their meaning, like so much in the dreamer's dictionary, depends on the dreamer's gender. To an unmarried woman aprons were thought to signify that she would meet and eventually marry a wealthy man, but that for the marriage to be successful she would have to use all her skills and wiles to keep him. To a married woman, the appearance of an apron promised that her children would be a source of immense pride once they had completed their education and embarked on their careers. To male dreamers who see themselves wearing an apron it suggests that a great deal of diplomatic skill is going to be needed to extricate themselves from a potentially embarrassing situation. If someone else is wearing an apron then that person may soon be looking to the dreamer for protection.

Arenas signify that the dreamer must face the fact that a decision has to be made that will involve a move into a new, specially created environment: perhaps an employer is so impressed with him or her that a new position has been envisaged specifically with the dreamer in mind. They can also be an expression of an

• •

awareness that some sort of conflict that has been lingering in the background for some time should be brought out into the open and dealt with if it is not to fester like a bad wound and seep into other, at present non-involved areas of the dreamer's life.

Assassins are as unwelcome in dreams as they are in real life for to dream of being killed by one says that try as you might, whatever you strive for will never be achieved. To see someone else being assassinated, and if there is fresh blood on the body, is a warning that an enemy will play a particularly dirty trick on the dreamer to bring him low. Assassins also warn that unknown enemies may be about to cause the dreamer considerable financial loss. If the dreamer is a woman, the presence of an assassin in her dreams suggests that she is scared that something she had hoped would remain secret for ever may be about to be revealed and that the revelation will cause her considerable embarrassment and distress.

Autopsies, unpleasant as they may be in real life, are welcome when seen in dreams where they point to new and interesting experiences down the road (often of a sexual nature).

Autumn has little meaning in the male dream landscape, but when it colours the dreams of a woman, she is being told that she will gain some sort of advantage – maybe a financial windfall – not through her own efforts, but through the hard work of others. If she is unmarried and sees herself an autumn bride, then her marriage will be a good one and she will have an especially happy home life.

Avalanches suggest that while we may feel we are coping with life, deep down we fear that we are being overwhelmed. So, in that context, they are telling the dreamer that he or she should take steps to regain control of outside forces. Another interpretation is that obstacles are about to crash into the dreamer's life and there is absolutely nothing that can be done about them. Oddly, though, if the dreamer sees him or herself being buried in an avalanche, spectacular good fortune may be on its way. If others are being swept away in a landslide then a change in surroundings is indicated.

Babies' rattles, to young women, herald an early marriage and that babies will be quick to follow. To others, they say that little will shake the dreamer's

● ●

contentment, that home life will be happy, and that on the job front, things will go well.

Bailiffs suggest that the dreamer has serious doubts as to his or her abilities to manage their resources and is increasingly aware that they may have gone too far in some respect of their lives and are fearful that they may be about to be held accountable for doing so. Bailiffs also indicate that we suspect we have not fulfilled our obligations as efficiently as we might have and have put ourselves at risk, which will cause us material loss unless we take responsibility for our actions. To Romany folk, the appearance of bailiffs said that the dreamer was striving to get on in life, but that a lack of intellect would hold him back. And if the bailiff marched the dreamer off (or in the case of women, made love to them!) then that was a warning that acquaintances who pretended to be friends were scheming to impoverish the dreamer in some way.

Bait being laid by a woman to trap or lure a household pest is seen as her having serious doubts in her ability to attract a suitable partner, and because of this she feels that she may have to resort to trickery to find herself happily settled. To dreamers of both sexes, bait can also be an indication that something that has been kept hidden needs to be brought out into the open if their full potential is to be achieved. To do this, some sort of self-help techniques may have to be resorted to. On a spiritual level, the dream may suggest that before anything seen as evil in the dreamer's life can be discarded, it may have to be 'trapped' in some way.

Balance, in the waking world, can be taken two ways: it can have either a physical or financial meaning. If we dream that we are trying to maintain our balance, then the interpretation is quite straightforward – something is out of kilter in our lives and we are struggling to find a way to regain our equilibrium. If the dream concerns balancing our finances then we are acknowledging that we are lacking something in our lives but that we are not sure what that something is. If the dream concerns balance in a mercantile sense – i.e. we have been shortchanged – then the dreamer may be awakening to the fact that he has a good deal more intelligence than either he is or the people he knows are aware of.

Baldness in other people is an acknowledgement that the dreamer is growing ever more aware that his or her life is becoming increasingly dull. It can also suggest that someone may be working against the dreamer in some way, but he won't succeed as long

● ●

as the dreamer keeps his wits about him. On a deeper level, baldness is a recognition that the dreamer is concerned about the spiritual side of life and would like to pay it more attention. And according to folklore, to dream of a bald-headed woman suggests that his wife will turn out to be a real shrew, if she has not proved to be so already.

Balloons, long-time symbols of joy and happiness, suggest that the dreamer is looking for joy and happiness of a sexual rather than a spiritual nature. But as they have also been said to suggest that hopes will be blighted and that business is heading for a downturn – you pays your money and takes your choice!

Banks are thought to point to a need for spiritual security and on a more practical level to a growing awareness that financial affairs may need to be put on more secure footing if the dreamer is to be able to look forward to a secure future. If the dreamer is in a bank and sees that there is no one ahead in the queue, then according to one august dream expert of days gone by, business losses loom large.

Baptism is indicative of a new influence entering the dreamer's life and that he or she is aware that it's time to get the new broom out and start to sweep clean, especially in long-held attitudes to life. Baptism can also suggest an unspoken yet deeply felt resentment that the dreamer was forced to accept religious beliefs that are now felt to be a hindrance. It can also warn the dreamer to keep his or her opinions to themselves or risk provoking an argument with friends.

Baskets, as long as they are full, tell the dreamer that unqualified success lies ahead in anything to which the dreamer wants to turn his or her hand. But if they are empty, discontentment and sorrow cloud the horizon. To be seen trying to fill an empty basket suggests that the dreamer wants to increase his or her talents and abilities but is not sure how to go about doing so.

Bays (of a topographical kind) are seen as symbolic of a woman's sexuality, the female dreamer's acceptance of it, and the male dreamer's acknowledgement that he is receptive to it. Keeping something at bay, tells the dreamer to keep their wits about them if they are to avoid being duped in some way. And to hear an animal baying says that the dreamer is well aware of his or her animal instincts and their willingness, indeed eagerness, to overcome them. On an equestrian level, to see oneself riding a bay mare suggests that a male dreamer will

● ●

experience an upturn in fortune and that his sexual fantasies may be about to be gratified in the flesh. To the female dreamer, being atop such a mount says that her enjoyment of material things will see her giving in to the sexual advances of a predatory male.

Beaches are an expression of the dreamer's awareness that there is a boundary between the emotional and the real and that if they acknowledge this when awake, life will run much more smoothly. Beaches also tell the dreamer to come down to Earth – literally, and that if he or she becomes more in tune with the elements then life will be all the better for it. Beaches can, depending on what the dreamer is doing on them and his or her state of mind at the time of the dream, indicate a need to relax more and to express the more creative side of their nature. If there is no one on the beach, then some interpreters see this as a sign that if the dreamer has been searching for the emotional clarity to solve a problem, the search may soon be over.

Beacons say that the dreamer is aware that unless he makes himself aware of what is going on around him at all times, things could start to go wrong in his life. The signs that this is necessary have already been noted in the deep recesses of the mind, but have not yet registered in the conscious mind. They suggest to some interpreters that the dreamer's emotions are about to take control and lead him into dangerous waters unless they can be brought under control and the reasons acknowledged and rationalized. On another level, a beacon can be indicative of the fact that the dreamer has made the decision to let the spiritual side of life play a large part and is telling him that this was the correct decision. To seers of old, the appearance of a beacon indicated that the winds of good fortune were blowing in the dreamer's direction and that prosperity lay ahead. Beacons were also thought to say that dreamers who were suffering from ill health would soon be on the road to recovery and to businessmen that an upturn was on the cards. But to see one being extinguished or going out, said that just when you thought there was plain sailing ahead, Fate had decided to have the last laugh.

Being barefoot was traditionally held to warn that the dreamer's every expectation will be crushed, and that evil influences lie round every corner. Being shoeless can also be an expression of the need for sensual freedom.

Bereavement is something that happens in all our lives and consequently occasionally turns up in our dreams. A clinical interpretation of such a dream is that while the dreamer may seem to have come to terms with a disappointment, a loss or a setback, the full effects have yet to make themselves apparent. In earlier times, to dream of being bereaved was thought to be a warning that long-laid plans might prove to be fruitless, no matter how successful they appeared to be at that moment. And if the dreamer sees him or herself bereft of a close relative, then such plans will *definitely* flounder.

Bibles indicate that the dreamer is aware of the part that traditional moral codes can play in life and that the time has come to adopt a code of conduct that will help one mentally to survive the stress of early-twenty-first-century living. To Gypsies the appearance of the Bible in a dream presaged innocent pleasure. But to be denying the teachings of the Good Book was seen as a warning that the dreamer was about to be seduced from the path of righteousness.

Biting or **being bitten** has several meanings depending on who is doing the biting and what is being bitten into! Being bitten by someone we recognize tells us that we know we are the victim of some sort of aggressive behaviour but are not sure how to cope with it. Conversely, it can mean that the dreamer is not sure how to handle his or her own aggressive tendencies. To see oneself biting into something such as a fruit has a very literal interpretation: that is we should put our teeth into an opportunity that has recently presented itself. To dream of being bitten by a dog, used to be thought of as a warning that quarrels with a business partner or spouse lay ahead. To be bitten by a flea said that slander was in the air and if a spider was seen to bite the dreamer, then he or she would suffer as the result of someone being unfaithful either in business or socially.

Brothels featuring in a man's dream suggest a deep-rooted fear of being seen as feminine and a reluctant awareness that all males owe a spiritual debt to women. If the dreamer is female, then to dream of being in a brothel suggests that she has not yet come to terms with the fact that sex is there to be enjoyed and is not to be seen as a duty. To Gypsies, a dreamer seeing himself in a brothel says that the pursuit of material possessions will lead to terrible disgrace.

Cemeteries with their obvious associations with death have a double, indeed treble, psychological significance. They can represent parts of the dreamer that he has discarded or simply stopped using, either knowingly or unknowingly, something that was once an important part of his being. They can also, perhaps more obviously, signify that the dreamer is increasingly aware of his mortality and his attitude towards it. A third interpretation is that when cemeteries appear in our dreams, we are giving ourselves permission to show our fear of something, not necessarily death, important to us. On a more fanciful level, to see an immaculately well-kept cemetery, its gravestones free from weeds and with its grassy areas neatly trimmed, presages that someone you have given up for dead (perhaps not physically but with whom there had been no contact for such a long time that he or she has been forgotten) is about to reappear in your life. Romanies believed that to see such a dream signifies that property that had been lost to a usurper was about to be returned. And continuing with such interpretations, to see an ill-tended cemetery means that the dreamer will live to see loved ones desert him and leave him to spend his final years in the care of strangers. But for young people to see themselves strolling along line after line of gravestones is thought to signify that their friends would be a great source of comfort to them in times of sorrow which are, sadly, unavoidable. Engaged women who saw themselves being married in a dream cemetery were, in days gone by, believed to be being warned that their spouses (when they eventually married them) would meet a fatal accident while on a journey far from home. Good news, though, for married women to dream they are walking through a burial ground clasping a large bunch of flowers. Gypsies believed (and still do) that such a dream was a sign that family members were destined to enjoy robust good health all of their lives. And for women in mourning for their dead husbands to dream of being in a cemetery presaged that black clothes would soon be exchanged for some of a colour more suited to a woman being married a second time!

And to finish on two pieces of good news heralded by dreams of cemeteries. First for old people. If burial places feature in your dreams, then especially pleasant journeys lie ahead at the end of which you will be perfectly rested and invigorated. Second, dreaming of young children picking flowers from a graveyard was traditionally regarded as a sign that the winds of prosperity were about to blow in the dreamer's direction.

Cherubs say that the dreamer is going to go through a particularly happy phase in his or her life, the memory of which will stay forever. That is if they are smiling

• •

beatifically. If they are frowning or in any other way looking displeased, then the dreamer is about to hear some particularly depressing news.

Churchyards have three main meanings. First the bad news! To dream of strolling through one that is covered with a coating of snow crisp underfoot denotes that if poverty is to be avoided, then a huge effort will have to be made. And in avoiding penury, the dreamer may have to leave family and friends behind and go and live far away – at least for a little while. Next the not quite so bad news. If the dreamer is female, in love and sees herself in a churchyard it is an indication that she and her love will never share the marital bed with each other and that true happiness lies with someone else. And now for the good news: if spring is obviously in the air then friends will make life especially pleasant in the immediate future and the opportunity to travel to new, exciting and extremely beautiful places is about to present itself.

Clocks alert the dreamer to the passage of time, perhaps to an awakening that we are all mortal, or maybe clocks signify an awareness that the time is right to do something that we have been putting off doing and which has now acquired a sense of urgency.

Closeness in the physical rather than the weather sense suggests that the dreamer is growing increasingly aware that there is a need for intimacy and/or protection. If this is not satisfied in the near future, then the dreamer will become more and more afraid that the future will be lonely and perhaps unsafe.

Clover, a traditional symbol of good luck in life, is just as lucky in dreams, where it signifies that Dame Fortune is arranging things to the dreamer's benefit. To dream of it in any of its many leafed varieties can also suggest that the dreamer is concerned that the various parts that go to make up his whole are out of tune with each other and that for harmony to be restored the scales must be rebalanced.

Clubs, the sort which our prehistoric ancestors used as weapons, are seen as symbolic of violence lying deep within us. This has probably been dormant and unexpressed for years, perhaps since childhood, but is now surfacing in the dreamer's subconscious and may be about to make its presence felt in the waking as well as the sleeping life. Clubs can also say that the dreamer harbours violent feelings about something for which he has never been able to forgive himself. They can also say that the dreamer possesses enormous strength which has yet to be channelled properly.

• •

Clubs, in the social sense, indicate the desire that we all have to belong. If we see ourselves as having a good time and mixing well with others then it's probable that we see ourselves as part of society as a whole. But if we are lingering like wallflowers at the back of the border, then this suggests that we see ourselves as being separate from our peers, and that we are not sure why this should be. However, like all problems, the solution or part of it lies in recognizing that there is a problem in the first place. Once the dreamer acknowledges this, he or she can take the appropriate steps to remedy it.

Coffins are a reminder that all men are mortal and that the dreamer is no exception. They also say that he or she is coming to terms with some sort of loss, perhaps the death of a relationship that was once central to the dreamer's life. They can also suggest that the dreamer is cutting off certain feelings and in doing so is allowing part of him or herself to die. For centuries, coffins have been seen as unlucky dream symbols. For farmers they were thought to warn of failed harvests and poor livestock, while to businessmen they were seen as a warning that debts were about to mount up and go out of control. To young dreamers, coffins warned that marital happiness was unlikely to be theirs, at least not with their present partners! If the dreamer saw his or her own coffin, then there was gloom on both the domestic and the business fronts. And to see oneself sitting on a coffin was thought to be a warning that illness of a non-fatal nature was about to strike the dreamer.

Cold signifies neglect in the dream dictionary. To see oneself as being cold suggests that the dreamer feels left out of things.

Combs tidy our hair in our waking hours and when seen in dreams suggest that there is an as yet unacknowledged need to tidy up some aspect of our lives. Maybe it's our jobs that we need to pay some attention to, or a relationship that has gone a bit straggly at the edges and needs straightening out.

Comets flashing across a dream warn that the dreamer is afraid that there is a situation brewing which he or she knows will be impossible to control. What is going to happen is going to happen no matter what the dreamer does, so the only thing to do is prepare for the eventual flak, regardless of the direction in which it is scattered. That's one interpretation. Another is that the dreamer is puzzling over how to solve a problem and that the dream tells him that he should look for a practical solution rather than rely on a flash of inspiration.

A-Z OF DREAMS

• •

Compasses suggest that the dreamer needs help in charting his way through the immediate future. They [compasses] often appear when the dreamer has been presented with a set of choices and has no idea which one or ones to select. Another meaning that has been laid at compasses' door is that the dreamer feels that he or she has been the victim of some injustice and this is starting to impinge on rational thought when awake.

Computers (curse or blessing according to the dreamers' experiences of them) are new on the dream landscape, the first electronic one having been developed within the comparatively recent past. Interpreters are still not quite keyed in to their true meaning, but there is a growing consensus that they indicate that the dreamer is slowly coming round to the idea that he or she has untapped resources that could add to material and spiritual wellbeing. They may also suggest that every experience we have ever gone through since the moment we were born (maybe even since the moment when the first brain cells developed in the foetus) has been stored and is there to be rediscovered and evaluated.

Conch shells, with their beautiful spiral shape and luminescent linings lend themselves to ideas of perfection in real life. In dreams they suggest that the dreamer is gradually becoming aware that life need not be as dull as a 1950s' Scottish Sunday and that a little Saturday Night Fever is good for the spirits. Some societies in which the conch shell was (and may still be) used as a trumpet think that to dream of one serves as a warning of some kind. They may be right. And with that in mind, perhaps the dreamer who sees one should remember the old maxim, 'Forewarned is forearmed.'

Cooking can tell the dreamer that they have a hunger that is demanding to be satisfied – not necessarily a physical hunger, perhaps an emotional one or a craving to make use of opportunities that have presented themselves but that have been sidelined for the time being. To see oneself as cooking can be the subconscious's way of telling the dreamer to take such opportunities out of the shunting yard and get them back on the rails before it's too late. To be preparing food can also be the mind's way of telling the dreamer that he or she has all the ingredients for success and that if only the right recipe is found, the future can be faced with increased confidence.

Corners need to be turned in dreams as well as in life, and when we see ourselves going round one, it is probable that we are congratulating ourselves for

● ●

having surmounted some obstacles and coming
through as stronger, more capable people. If, however,
we see ourselves approaching one in our dreams,
then it indicates that there is a problem coming up. If it
is a left-handed one, then the answer to it probably lies
in using intuition rather than acting logically. If the
corner is right-handed, then the dreamer should follow
logic rather than emotion to get round it. Corners can
also suggest that the dreamer has been living a lie for
some time – not necessarily a thundering whopper,
maybe just a tiny white one. The dream says that the
dreamer is coming close to acknowledging that the
time is right to come clean or else he or she will feel
trapped in a web of deceit for ever. Anyone in this
situation who sees a corner coming up or being
turned, should remember that you can fool all of the
people some of the time and you can fool some of the
people all of the time. But you cannot fool all of the
people all of the time.

Corpses have a variety of meanings. The most
common interpretation, especially among sages of
days gone by, is an obvious one that when a corpse
appears in a dream, the sad – very sad – news will be
received concerning an absent friend. For businessmen
such a dream warns that the good times may be over
– for ever. And to young dreamers, corpses herald that

the immediate future is unlikely to be marked by happiness! If the dead body is being placed in a coffin by the undertaker's men, it suggests imminent unspecified troubles for the dreamer. Lovers dreaming of dead bodies is thought to be a sure sign that promises made will turn out to be promises broken. If the corpse is animal rather than human, then the dreamer's health is under threat – not necessarily physical health: it is perhaps to spiritual or financial health that the dreamer should turn his or her attention.

Cranes, the ones seen on building sites rather than the feathered variety, tell the dreamer that it is time to raise awareness about something that has been lurking in the dark recesses of the mind for some time. It's likely that the dreamer has been focusing on distracting detail – the dream tells him that it's time to see the bigger picture. They also say that if he puts his mind to something, he should be able to put himself in the driving seat and turn a situation to his advantage.

Daggers when seen being used offensively by the dreamer suggest he or she harbours a desire to cut something out of his or her life, which has come to be seen as redundant. If the weapon is being used against the dreamer, then it is likely that a feeling of vulnerability is being acknowledged.

A-Z OF DREAMS

• •

Dams tell dream analysts that emotions are being bottled up and could break through at any time with devastating effect on the dreamer's life. They can also suggest that the dreamer suspects that someone else may be about to let his emotions fly in the dreamer's direction and that he or she would rather this did not happen. To be seen building a dam is indicative that the dreamer is shoring up his defences lest some hurt be about to upset his equilibrium. And if a dam is seen to burst, then the dreamer is expressing a fear that he or she knows no way to control the emotions of close members of the family.

Darkness warns that in the immediate future work will not go well. But if the sun breaks through, things will pick up very soon. If the dream concerns searching for someone in the dark, then you will be provoked by trivialities into losing your temper with dramatic results. Keep your cool and you should be OK. Lose it and look out! If you dream that you are groping around in a strange place in the dark, then you may be about to get an urgent summons to somewhere you have never been before where sorrow of some kind waits to welcome you.

Dawns are as welcome in dreams as they are after long, dark nights, as long as they are bright and clear,

330

● ●

for they say that business is set for success and the dreamer can look forward to the immediate future with confidence. But if the sky is overcast, then dull routine will wear the dreamer down to the point that life becomes a drudge.

Days, when they appear in the dreamer's sleeping mind, herald an all-round boost in life: business will go well, job prospects will pick up and any hints of disharmony on the home front will vanish. Unless that is, the day is gloomy and overcast, for in that case a new enterprise that looked promising will prove the old saying that all that glistens is not gold!

Demolition has been reported surprisingly often as a dream theme. Its meaning depends on who is doing the demolishing. If it's the dreamer, then he or she is expressing a need to be in control in most situations. The dreamer is often the sort of person who seems to be driven by ambition, but is impossible to work with unless he (and the dreamer is usually a male) is in the boss's chair. If someone else is doing the demolishing, then the dreamer is acknowledging his awareness that other people control the most important elements of his life, and if there are to be changes, no matter how unpleasant, there is little the dreamer feels can be done about them.

A-Z OF DREAMS

Devouring has a different meaning from eating (see Menu of Dreams). In devouring dreams people often see themselves as being devoured by something or someone, as opposed to enjoying a burger and fries! When the former is experienced, the dreamer is expressing a deeply-rooted but not expressed fear of losing his or her identity because of developing some sort of obsession.

Draughts are an indication that the dreamer is aware of being in a position where external forces over which he or she has little control could be about to blow the winds of change through their lives. Draughts are often reported in the dreams of those who work in industries or businesses that are unusually susceptible to sudden changes in market forces and where having what seems to be a very secure job on a Monday is no guarantee that a redundancy cheque won't be paid into the bank by Friday. To be seen to be creating a draught on the other hand suggests that the dreamer is the type of person who will always act as peacemaker when disputes threaten to ruffle feathers.

Droughts are not to be welcomed during our sleeping hours! Family squabbles will deepen into serious arguments that could take years to settle.

Droughts also herald ill health heading the dreamer's way and that plans that looked as if they had been built on firm foundations will turn out to be have been built on shifting sands! Farmers used to dread dreaming of drought because according to rural folklore, such a dream served as a warning that some of their livestock may be about to meet with a fatal accident.

Dusk, sadly, says that hopes are about to be dashed on the rocks of disappointment – especially if they concern business or career. Unmarried women who are seeing someone 'on the side' and who dream that they are walking hand in hand with their paramours in the dusk can wave goodbye to secrecy! Their secret is about to be blown.

Earthquakes used to be regarded as a sign that nation would make war unto nation! Today, they are more likely to denote business failure. If your house is seen to shake during an earthquake, then some sort of official announcement could be about to affect your property. To married women, dream earthquakes are thought to herald good news. But to dream of an earthquake when there may have been a little hiccup in the workplace suggests that a jealous colleague caused it. And if the land is seen to split during an earthquake, then according to one sage of the dim and distant past, you could be in danger of being trapped in a fire.

Eclipses, solar eclipses that is, are indicative that the dreamer holds deep-rooted fears about the direction life is taking and is concerned that success may always be elusive. Colleagues and friends, the dreamer thinks, seem to have achieved some degree of importance because they give an impression of being more able than he is, something that prevents him from showing his true potential. Eclipses also often feature in dreams at times when the dreamer is putting a brave face on things and feels that this may not be possible for much longer. Dream interpreters of the past thought that to dream of an eclipse served as a warning that the dreamer should mend his ways and curb his excesses if his health was not to suffer. A lunar eclipse, on the other hand, said that if the dreamer could keep his head when all around were losing theirs, he would be unaffected by an oncoming unpleasantness.

Education, with its obvious connection to school and university, says to dreamers that the time has come to be more disciplined than they have been of late if they are not to be seen to be performing inadequately either in career or family matters. It also says that lessons learnt in the past, if applied to the present and future, could provide considerable benefits. On a more superficial level, to dream of education could indicate that the dreamer sees a better education as the key to success. Ninety-nine times out of a hundred, this could be true, but there's always that one percent!

Eggs are thought to be symbolic of the dreamer's awareness that there are huge reserves of potential that have still to be tapped. They also say that before he or she can enjoy life to the full, part of which can only be achieved if that potential is fully realized, planning will be all-important. And as part of this planning progress, the dreamer may have to withdraw, monk-like, into the cell of his own mind for a while and emerge, butterfly-like as a new being. Fortune-tellers of old believed that to dream of a nest of eggs was a sign that financial gains were in view. If the eggs were small, the windfall would be similarly tiny but would come at a time of great need and would still be seen as a blessing. And if the eggs were cracked, the good fortune would drift out of the dreamer's life to be replaced by disappointment. Bright, shiny eggs heralded a happy event in the family.

A-Z OF DREAMS

• •

Electricity, unknown to sages two centuries ago, is a comparatively recent arrival on the dream stage. With its associations with power, it says to the dreamer that we all have the power to make a contribution to life and it is up to us to find out what it is. If we grab it, we just may leave a footstep in the sands of time, but if we let it slip from our grasp, our lives will go unmarked by future generations. If the dreamer sees himself as being electrocuted or suffering an electric shock he is being told to be on the alert if he is not to fall victim to some sort of danger.

Escape tells us that the dreamer is keen to avoid a difficult situation about to present itself, or wants to move on from one that has already arrived. It may be that the dreamer is in a position of some responsibility, which he is finding onerous and would like to relinquish. Some dream interpreters think that the escape dream is most often experienced by people who found their childhood so intolerable that they have spent their adult lives trying to leave it behind, but are constantly haunted by their demons. Gypsies believed, and still do, that to dream of escaping from jail meant a rapid rise up the career ladder, while to escape from the clutches of a wild animal suggested that the dreamer should be on the alert lest the schemes of a false friend land him in trouble.

A MISCELLANY OF DREAMS

Evenings suggest that hopes and plans that the dreamer has come to think would never be realized will suddenly be back on the agenda and will come to happy fulfilment. If there are stars shining in the evening sky, then there may be trouble ahead, but if you face the music and dance, you'll soon put it behind you. But to see yourself walking hand in hand with your lover in the evening twilight is a suggestion that night may be about to fall on your relationship – for a short while at least.

Fables can indicate several things to the dream interpreter. They can say that dull labour is a thing of the past and that the future is filled with pleasant duties. They can also suggest that the dreamer has a talent for writing that has not yet been exploited. If the fables dreamed of are religious in nature, then the dreamer may be slowly awakening to the fact that the spiritual side of life has been neglected. To dream of being part of a fable, is to be warned that there is too much pretence in the dreamer's life and that ostrich-like he has his head buried in the sand. It is time, the dream is saying, to wake up and face the truth about something, no matter how unpleasant it may be. And to dream of fabulous beasts such as unicorns suggests that the dreamer has been trying to reconcile two sides of an argument – and has failed to do so.

● ●

Failure of a personal nature is dreamed of by people of a highly competitive nature who fear that they are being seen by their peers as performing inadequately – not necessarily in the workplace, but more often than not in the bedroom. If the dream recurs then the dreamer is being warned that this fear of failure is clouding all his judgement. Dreamers who experience this should come to understand that we can't be successful all the time and that into every life a little failure must fall.

Fakirs, not especially common, but noteworthy nonetheless for their suggestion that many changes lie in store. They also, perhaps more obviously suggest that the dreamer is increasingly aware on a subconscious level that friends who have suggested that they can help in some way have yet to put their money where their mouths are – and perhaps never will.

Fame suggests that the dreamer is a shrinking violet when it comes to recognizing his or her own abilities. Deep down, of course, dreamers know what their true potential is, and to see themselves as famous in their dreams is compensation for their failure to achieve it in real life. Gypsy tradition holds that to dream of being famous is to be warned to expect some sort of reversal, especially in business.

A MISCELLANY OF DREAMS

● ●

Films seen in dreams can be quite spooky – a bit like watching a play within a play. One interpretation of them is that the dreamer is aware that something belonging to the past needs to be taken off the shelf, dusted down and reinterpreted if he is to really come to terms with its effect on his life. To dream of sitting in the director's chair or peering down the viewfinder of a movie camera (and one is not a movie director or a film cameraman!) is a suggestion that the life the dreamer is making for himself is not based in reality. To succeed, foundations will have to be dug deeper than they are at present.

Fire says that prosperity will warm your life, even if it is engulfing your home when it foretells that your choice of partner was, or will be, an excellent one and that your children will be as obedient as any children ever are. If the fire is spreading through the dreams of a businessman and burning down his shop or office, then the order books will soon be bursting and a period of prolonged prosperity will be enjoyed. But if he is fighting the fire and is unscathed, then the workload will become heavier than it has been of late, and there may be hiccups in the smooth running of the business. And if dreamers see themselves standing in the smouldering ruins of their business then such is the bad luck in store that they will be tempted to call it a

● ●

day. But they shouldn't despair, for a totally unexpected stroke of good fortune will soon have them back on their feet again. If the fire is of a domestic nature, and the dream concerns sitting by the fireside, kindling the coals, then an unexpected visit from some long unseen friends is about to happen.

Fire engines racing to an emergency, lights blazing and sirens wailing, warn that the dreamer is about to be hit by some totally unexpected event that will see fortune not so much smiling but positively beaming on the dreamer. But if they are seen by an unmarried woman, her behaviour may be about to be called into question. Some dreamers have taken the appearance of a fire engine in their dreams as a warning to make sure their fire insurance is in order – and have been glad that they did so!

Floods are as disastrous to the dreamer as they can be in real life, for to dream that you are being swept along in a flood that is destroying huge areas of the country is to be warned that your health is about to go on a downward slope. Not just that! Your business could be heading for the rocks along with your marriage! If the flood turns into what can only be called an inundation of dirty water, then that suggests a bereavement. But if the water is clear, then after a spell when the dreamer thinks that things just can't get worse, he's quite right. They will pick up and the waters of despair will recede to be replaced by the rays of bright sunshine. An old interpretation of dreaming of floods was that people richer than the dreamer will cause him problems and it could be that a wealthy rival in love is about to steal a march on him.

Friends can have an obvious meaning in dreams. If a friend has been in our thoughts, then he or she is quite liable to pop up in the dream world at any time. But of course, they have a deeper meaning. If we dream of the same friend over and over again, then perhaps the subconscious is suggesting that the time has come to examine the friendship and what it really means to us. It may be that we have come to see the person as being rather more than a friend. Or that friendship has slipped to the Christmas card level and the dreamer must decide whether or not to make the conscious effort to revive it, or to let it become a pleasant acquaintanceship rather than a true friendship. On a slightly more fanciful level, the appearance of good friends in a dream heralds good news concerning either them or a close relative. If the friends dreamed of appear to be especially friendly, then current activities will be particularly successful. If, however, the friends are sad or unhappy, then you can expect to

● ●

receive news that someone you know has been stricken with illness.

Funerals warn of an unhappy marriage and that any offspring will be puny and whingy children who, if they survive into adulthood, will be puny and whingy adults! That is if the person being buried is known to the dreamer: if not then the interment denotes that unexpected worries are about to descend. If a woman sees herself as dressed in black and following a funeral cortege, then according to Gypsy belief any fears she has of early widowhood will come true. And if parents of either sex see themselves attending the funeral of one or other of their children, a friend with good intentions will raise hopes high only to dash them on the rocks of disappointment shortly afterwards. On a deeper level, to dream of being at a funeral is thought to be an indication that the dreamer needs to come to terms with their attitude towards death. It can also indicate that the time has come to bury memories of some sad or disappointing event and move on. And to dream of one's own funeral suggests that the dreamer feels that he deserves sympathy for something and is disappointed that it is not forthcoming. And before the subject is buried, to dream of one's parent's death is an indication that the dreamer feels that it is time to assert

• •

his or her independence and to say goodbye to childish
things and accept the responsibilities of adulthood.

Garbage indicates that it is time for the dreamer to
give life a good spring clean. Memories of experiences
that have been holding us back should be discarded
so that we can move on. Those from which we can
learn, should be taken off the shelf, dusted down and
re-examined for the potential they still hold. Garbage,
especially if the sort of kitchen debris that older readers
may recall as being set aside for pig swill, can be the
body's (and the brain is a part of the body) way of
telling us that we should take time out to make sure
that we are doing everything we can to maintain our
health. As one interpreter writes, 'It's an omen to
change your ways before you turn all the lovely things
with which you were blessed into ****.' To dream that
you are collecting garbage can say that you are
starting to doubt some of the assumptions on which
you have founded your life – especially your moral
code. And if you dream that you are disposing of
garbage, then you may be concerned that you will
be asked to defend someone whose reputation
has become tainted by the mess he is making
of his life.

● ●

Gas has among its meanings one very sensible one. If
you dream that you smell gas, then the chances are
that it is not a dream, but that your 'sleeping' brain is
registering that you are actually smelling gas and is
warning you to wake up! Even if the merest whiff is
smelt, then first thing on waking have all your
appliances checked. And if, when you wake up there
is a strong smell of gas, open a window and don't
whatever you do light a match or even put on an
electric light. The slightest spark can ignite gas fumes
and cause an explosion. Otherwise, its appearance in
dreams is an indication that we are having difficulties in
controlling many aspects of our lives that we should
be able to reign in – our thoughts, feelings and how
we use our abilities mainly. Gas can also be an
acknowledgement of the power of the Spirit,
something to which the dreamer has probably given
little attention of late. Smelling gas and searching for
its source can suggest that friends are displeased
with you for some reason. Deep down, you know
what and the dream tells you that it is up to you to
make amends. And if the dream concerns cooking
with gas, then you can look forward to waving
adversity goodbye and giving the fruits of success
a warm welcome.

Glass represents the invisible barrier that we put between ourselves and the rest of the world to keep it at bay. It's something we all do, no matter how gregarious we see ourselves as being. And just as glass represents our barriers, it also represents other people's. Or as one cynic put it, glass says that we all know that self-defence is the best form of attack. If the glass is of the frosted or smoked variety then the dreamer has a 'DO NOT DISTURB' sign deeply engraved on his or her emotions. To dream that we are breaking glass is an expression of our awareness that if we all took down our barriers, then maybe, just maybe, we would all be better off for it. Trapped emotions could be set free and we could all relax and move on. Glass that has already been broken predicts that life is about to change – for the better if the glass is sparkling, for the worse if it's cloudy. If dreamers see themselves drinking out of gleamingly clean glasses, they are about to sip from the cup of good fortune.

Gongs being rung in our dreams announce either that a target set has now been reached, or if not reached we have gone as far as we can go towards achieving it and now must seek the approval of others before going any further. To see ourselves as striking a gong indicates our need for extra strength to see us through the immediate future. Such strength may be physical but is much more likely to be emotional. Gongs can also serve as an alarm call to wake us up to the fact that we have been neglecting the spiritual side of life and that if we are to be seen by our peers as well-rounded people, we need to pay it significant attention.

Guillotines feature more in the dreams of those who live in countries where they were once used as a means of capital punishment. But we are all aware of what they are and although not common they do appear in our dreams. When they do, they may indicate a fear of lack of self-control or loss of dignity, or a dislike of anything to which we cannot give a logical explanation when it enters our lives. They can indicate an awareness of the potential to cut ourselves off from those we love, or indeed that we have lost the capacity to love altogether. To paraphrase the hero of Charles Dickens' A Tale of Two Cities – there are far, far better dreams to dream – but there are far, far worse ones, too.

Haggard faces in a dream are two warnings in one! Firstly, they have been noted many times as having appeared in the dreams of those who a little later wake up to realize that their love life is heading for disaster and there is nothing they can do about it, for when the realization sets in, it's too late. And there are almost as

• •

many instances of such faces being seen by dreamers who later find that their businesses are in a precarious state of affairs. If it's your own face that appears lined, worried and aged, then keep a look out over your shoulder for ill health. If the dream is accompanied by a feeling of being tired, that's a warning to slow down, you're going too fast.

Halters suggest that the dreamer has been keeping too tight a rein on his intellect, and that if only he could find the courage to loosen it, he would gallop ahead, especially in creative matters. Even those who are about as creative as a dead sheep should think what such a creature becomes in the hands of artist Damien Hirst, and they could be surprised at what they might achieve if they take the dream as a suggestion to try and be a little more imaginative. To dream of putting a halter on a horse denotes that the dreamer is looking for someone to show him the way to a life of deeper spiritual satisfaction. And in Gypsy tradition, to see a young horse being put to the halter for the first time, is to be told that a recently made acquaintance will put a business proposition the dreamer's way, and he (the dreamer) would do well to consider it seriously.

Harems, the stuff of which many male dreams are made, may make the male dreamer seem macho when he sees himself strutting among his concubines, but in fact analysts believe that such a dream is a sign that he is aware he has a feminine side but that he is struggling to come to terms with its complexities. To women dreamers, seeing themselves in a harem is indicative that they are totally at ease with their sensual nature, indeed enjoy it considerably. Such a dream can also suggest that the dreamer feels a need for the companionship of other women, perhaps to be part of a sorority with the members of which she can share problems and common experiences. More romantic interpretations say that the dreamer is being warned that he is wasting his energies in the pursuit of belittling pleasures. But the leopard can change its spots and if the energies are properly channelled then the dreamer's true promise and potential can, and will, be realized. On the same level, if a woman dreams such a dream, she may be tempted to indulge in adultery. If she sees herself as favourite concubine she will be offered the chance to indulge in material pleasures – but the opportunity will soon be whisked away from her and she will come down to Earth with a bang.

Hieroglyphics, the meaning of which was lost to us from Ancient Egyptian times until the early nineteenth-century when the symbols were successfully interpreted, foretell of hardships experienced while deciding which career path to follow. But if you dream that you read these strange pictograms and understand what they say, then the obstacles that will be put in your path will be temporary and easily overcome on your way to considerable success.

Historical settings indicate that the dreamer feels the need to get in touch with his or her past in order to come to terms with something that is clouding the sunshine today. Some interpreters believe that the earlier the setting, the farther back the dreamer has to go to get to the root of the problem, but that may be putting too literal an interpretation on things. The dream can also be a sign that the dreamer looks on the way things were with fond nostalgia and wishes that the clock could somehow be turned back.

Hooks tell the dreamer that deep inside him, he has the power to draw things to him, and that it is up to him whether to use this ability for the general good or otherwise. Or, to see a hook can indicate that the dreamer feels that he has been unfairly lured to do something that would normally have gone against his nature or instincts, and that in being so hooked he is

afraid that his freedom has been severely restricted.
Travelling folk believe that to dream of a hook means to
be burdened by unhappy duties.

Hurricanes have various meanings – none of them
good! To hear or see one heading your way suggests
that you are going to have your work cut out to survive
a downturn in business. To be in a house that is being
buffeted by hurricane-force winds you may have to
flee to far-off places to avoid some sort of business or
emotional disaster. And it may be that no matter how
far you go, your past will forever be snapping at your
heels. If you see yourself looking at the aftermath of a
terrible hurricane, you will sail close to the winds of
disaster but a white knight will ride to your rescue at
the very last minute. To see dead bodies being
dragged from the havoc caused by a hurricane says
that the troubles of another, probably a family member,
will cause you great distress. To dream of a hurricane
can serve as a warning that you will be dragged into a
legal dispute in which you have no real involvement but
that both parties will try to get you on their side. Best to
stay neutral and avoid the recriminations that are
certain to follow if you do get involved.

Ice can say that the dreamer sees himself as being
something of a cold fish – and unless he can be seen

350

to be warmer in relationships with family and any friends that he may have made, they may give up on him. It can also indicate a failure to grasp the significance of what is happening all around and that this inability is creating an impression of being hopelessly out of touch. On a more ethereal level, ice can be seen as a sign that the dreamer has frozen out something concerning the past and that before he or she can move on, whatever it is has to be taken out of the freezer and put in the defrost compartment. Dark, dirty ice, Gypsies believe, augurs that bad feeling between friends could cause problems, or worse that you have innocently done something that has caused those who were previously indifferent to become filled with jealousy to such an extent that they are out to get you at any cost. To unmarried women, blocks of clear ice could presage becoming engaged in the near future. (This is an American interpretation and is likely to have come about because of the use of the word 'ice' as slang for diamonds.)

Icicles, when they hang from a wall, according to Shakespeare in *Love's Labour's Lost,* herald the owl's merry note. But to the dreamer, they suggest a feeling that support has been sadly lacking of late and that this has had a detrimental effect on things, particularly at work. To see them melting drip by drip says that

• •

troubles will likewise start to melt. And if they are seen to do this on the roof of the house means, according to Romany tradition, that marital troubles will end to be replaced by a long period of domestic harmony. The same tradition holds that to see them melting from trees suggests trouble of some sort concerning property. While to see them forming is a sign of troubles creeping up and catching the dreamer unawares, but that something equally unexpected will give him the ammunition to see them off.

Imitation can be seen as a sign that the dreamer is certain that the course of action that has been followed regarding a recent circumstance was the correct one, and that family, friends and colleagues alike should show some sign of gratitude. Being imitated in a dream can also suggest that the dreamer feels lacking in leadership skills despite being assured by others that he has them in spades. To see ourselves imitating one of our peers in a flattering fashion suggests that we have the conceit to believe that we could do just as good a job as they are doing regardless of the heights they have scaled. But if the person we are imitating is superior to us, then the dream is an acknowledgement that they have a deeper knowledge and understanding of things than we have – although that might change if we apply ourselves. If the imitation is intentionally unflattering then deep down we may be feeling that our behaviour of late has been lacking in integrity. Dream interpreters of times gone by believed that dreams featuring imitation served as a warning against being palmed off with something that would become a source of trouble. And if a girl dreamed that someone was imitating her lover, then the word 'fidelity' was one with which he was probably unfamiliar.

Infidelity, whether it is being seen as practised by dreamer or partner, serves as a warning to be more circumspect about your actions not just with each other but with the opposite sex in general. If the warning goes unheeded, the consequences could be considerable. To dream of being unfaithful with more than one other person is a sign of a guilty conscious, not necessarily in affairs of the heart.

Inventors are regarded as linking us with the more creative side of our nature, not in the artistic sense perhaps, but more likely that part that we all have that enables us to grasp an idea and give it practical vent. To see one in a dream suggests that the dreamer is slowly realizing this and is willing to be more flexible and receptive to new ideas. Another, perhaps more fanciful meaning handed down from generation to generation is that to dream of an inventor is to be told that an honour in recognition of a unique achievement will be bestowed on the dreamer. And to dream of actually inventing something denotes that aspirations to wealth and good fortune will be realized and that success will follow the dreamer in whichever direction he wishes to travel.

Jars are seen as concerned with the feminine and the maternal and are a sign that the dreamer is coming round to acknowledge the debt owed to both of these. It may be that holding back this recognition has prevented the dreamer developing into a complete person, and that this may now happen. Another interpretation is that when full, jars are synonymous with success and victory, but dreamed of as being empty denotes heartbreak and illness. A curious American interpretation is that to dream of foods usually sold in cans as being seen in jars is to be told that if frugality is practised for the time being, and that if any financial surpluses are saved rather than spent, the dividends they will yield will grow into significant sums. To dream of **being jarred** or shaken is an indication that while we may be moving forward in life, we are not firmly in the driver's seat and are consequently being put in a position where we may be hurt or knocked off our chosen path.

Jealousy of another's good fortune augurs that the dreamer's path to the top will be a risky affair and if the top job is achieved, then it will be an uncomfortable tenure as others will be constantly plotting to usurp the chairman's seat on the board. To be jealous of a spouse is to be warned that if enemies are not already plotting against you, they soon will be. If the dreamer is a young woman and she dreams that she is jealous of her lover, then a Gypsy seer would tell her that her swain's eyes are already wandering in another's direction.

Jubilees hold special significance for dreamers who believe that life goes in seven-year cycles. This makes the fiftieth year especially significant being the first year after the completion of seven such cycles. Dreams associated with such a celebration are thought, therefore, to indicate the successful completion of a rite of passage and the dawn of a new age. They also denote that the dreamer will be a participant in many pleasurable enterprises, especially if the dreamer is a young woman and the pleasurable enterprise she has on her mind is marriage. To dream of a religious jubilee was, according to Romany people, a sign that the dreamers would never travel far from home, and their lives would be unmarked by great unhappiness.

● ●

Juries suggest that the dreamer is keen to gain the approval of his peers and is afraid that he may struggle to achieve it, because they will fail to appreciate the motives that caused a certain choice to be made. If the dreamer sees himself being acquitted by twelve good men and true, then business is set to run smoothly. But if the verdict is 'Guilty!' he will be harassed by enemies to the point that his endurance will be tested to the limit. To see oneself as sitting on a jury was, according to tradition, a sign that job dissatisfaction was brewing and that it was time to explore new horizons on the career front. If we disagree with our fellow jurors, then we may be on the point of kissing convention goodbye and going our own way. And if we're in the majority, then we are happy with the course our life is taking and hope that no one rocks the boat.

Kaleidoscopes are an indication that the dreamer enjoyed the freedom that childhood offered while at the same time appreciated the disciplines that parents imposed. To dream of one in adulthood may be an acknowledgement that the dreamer has been indulging in too much freedom and that he would like someone to tell him to put the brakes on. They can also indicate an awareness that there is a reservoir of creative ability that is, as yet, untapped. And just as the designs that are seen through a kaleidoscope change every time the wheel is turned, so the dreamer feels a sense of awe every time the wheel of life turns and circumstances constantly change. But to dream of these constantly changing designs could mean that young dreamers are having a hard time making up their minds what to do with their lives. If the wheel settles on a particularly pleasing design, then not only will the dreamer make the right choice in career, their choice of lover will be the right one. But if the pattern is ugly and distorted, the future may hold more disappointments than can normally be expected.

Kegs have several meanings, depending on the state of the keg in question and how much it holds. To dream of one that seems to be in satisfactory condition is to be warned that there's a struggle ahead if the dreamer is to free himself from some sort of oppression. To see one that is cracked and leaking denotes that the immediate future will be scarred by family squabbles which if not settled could worsen. If the iron band that kept the struts together is loose, then married dreamers could be heading for the divorce courts if no action is taken to get back in step with one's partner. To dream of a full keg is to be told that the way you have chosen to approach a certain problem is the right one and that you should stick to it no matter what advice may be whispered in your ear. An empty one says exactly the opposite – if you want to overcome the problem change tactics – and the sooner the better.

Keys open the door to fresh opportunities. They do this by telling us to unlock memories that have been pushed to the furthest corners of our minds and to make us remember experiences and lessons that we had long forgotten. And they say that if we heed what they tell us then we will find the answers to many puzzling questions about who we are and how we have come to be where we are in life. And most exciting of all they tell us that if we use them, it's not too late to learn, to move on and to live a much more rewarding life. To dream of a bunch of keys is to have their message reinforced. To see yourself finding another's keys is to be told that domestic happiness is yours for the asking. But there is a downside to dreaming of keys. If we see ourselves as having lost them, then an unpleasant adventure of some sort is just around the corner. To see broken keys is to be told that married life will be marked by quarrels and long separations. And to give away keys in a dream is to be warned that poor judgement will lead to making many errors that could easily have been avoided.

● ●

Kisses of a gentle, loving nature being given to or by someone we love, are generally an omen of good that shows that the dreamer is at peace and happy contentment with himself. But if the kiss is unwelcome or from an illicit source then the dreamer may awake to find tongues wagging and that the immediate future is marred by a myriad of tiny vexations. Kissing someone we have known for some time may be a sign that something was holding us back from seeing them as true friends but whatever it was has now been removed and we finally accept the person for what they are. It can also suggest that the person we are kissing possesses a quality that we would like to have ourselves. As befits a culture that is more tactile than our own, Romany people have traditionally put several interpretations on kissing. They believe that to kiss children meant a happy family reunion and contentment in work, while kissing your mother was an indication of success and honours to come. To kiss an enemy presaged reconciliation, while to kiss a stranger suggested that the dreamer was possessed of a louche nature. To kiss someone on the neck said that a love of illicit passions coupled with weak self-discipline would lead to heartache for the people who held the dreamer in high regard. The list is almost endless – with different interpretations being put on who was being kissed and where the kiss was aimed! But perhaps the

• •

Romany interpretation could be summed up as to dream of enjoying a kiss properly bestowed on a person with whom one is properly acquainted is good news. Anything else usually spells trouble.

Kites recall the happy, carefree, irresponsible days of childhood. To dream of them is to acknowledge a need for spiritual freedom. They can also suggest that deep down the dreamer sees himself as something of a popinjay – and that there is a fear that someone will see through the bluster and reveal to all the shallow creature that lies beneath the façade. To dream of making a kite suggests that the dreamer will speculate a little in the hope of making a lot – and that all the 'littles' will soon start to mount to the gambler's disadvantage.

Knots present as many problems to the dream interpreter as they do to those who have to unravel them in real life. A common interpretation is that the simpler the knot, the greater the urgency to take a new direction in seeking the solution to a problem. And the more complicated it is, then the stronger the dreamer's feeling that it is only a sense of duty or even guilt that is keeping him or her bound to a certain situation. The way out of it is to loosen the ties, but the dream suggests a reluctance to do so. On a superficial level knots suggest that what appear to be trifling affairs are going to cause disproportionate problems: and to dream of tying a knot is indicative of the dreamer's independent nature and a stubborn refusal to give in to the nagging of an equally obstinate spouse or friend. Knots can suggest that the dreamer is facing what is seen as an insoluble problem. The dream is the subconscious's way of suggesting that a gradual approach is better than the one taken by Alexander the Great who when faced with the Gordian knot, unsheathed his sword and sliced through it!

Labels are associated with the deeply felt need that lies within all of us (despite appearances) to conform to society's mores. From birth, we are labelled with the names our parents give us, and when we dream of labels we are identifying with the need to name things, for without names and labels life wouldn't make sense. And so, to dream of labels is to acknowledge the search for order in your life. To dream of something being incorrectly labelled suggests awareness that we have failed to understand something correctly. Correspondingly, to dream of relabelling something is the subconscious's way of telling us that we have to put this right. To dream of reading a label suggests that you have let someone know your personal business or revealed your true feelings to them and this may have caused them considerable unhappiness.

Laboratories can indicate that the dreamer has an as yet unexpressed desire to approach life in a more logical and scientific way and in so doing wants to develop unexploited talents and abilities. The same dream might suggest an awareness that the dreamer is frittering time and energies in business ventures that are little better than mediocre. If the dream concerns an experiment that eventually fails, then your business may well follow suit. But if the experiment succeeds, then so too will career matters. If a breakthrough is seen to be made, a new idea will lead to totally unexpected and brilliant success.

Ladders often feature in the dreams of those who are in the throes of changing jobs. Hardly surprising when one thinks of the connections between the two – the dreamer is climbing the career ladder, ladders are used to move from one location to another and the dreamer is doing likewise. In this context they confirm that the dreamer believes that he is making the right move at the right time – as long as he is carrying the ladder and it is in perfect condition. If the rungs are broken, the transition may be difficult, and if someone else has the ladder, then the progress may depend on the help of colleagues. Ladders can also acknowledge that the time is right to make a move towards a more spiritual life. Interpretations from days gone by include that to see oneself falling from a ladder is a sign that present endeavours will be unsuccessful, and that if someone is steadying a ladder up which the dreamer is climbing, then the heights of the career ladder will be easily achieved.

Languages heard but not understood are a sign that we are aware that something is not right in our lives, but we are not quite sure what it is. They can also indicate a desire to let various aspects of our personalities play a more positive part in our lives – in other words, to speak for themselves. They can also suggest that the dreamer is having difficulties understanding the motives behind the actions of a good friend. In the days when classics were more widely taught in schools, Latin was thought to herald a victory or a distinction of some kind, while to dream of Greek suggested that the dreamer's ideas would be widely discussed and eventually accepted. Language of a foul sort is seen as a sign that the dreamer will soon find him or herself at the centre of an embarrassing situation brought about by another person's thoughtless actions.

A-Z OF DREAMS

● ●

Lotteries indicate that the dreamer may be of a lazy nature, especially in his job where he expects to be well paid for little effort. They can also suggest that he is the kind of person who will take a risk if he can see that the gain will far outweigh the input. Another interpretation is that carelessness could lead to disappointment. If the dream concerns losing a lottery, then beware lest false friends cause you to become the victim of circumstances. The news is not better if you dream of winning the lottery for in that case something unpleasant is on the cards. But if you dream that someone else has won, then fun times with friends lie ahead.

Machines may indicate a concern with the body's automatic functions: indeed it has been noted that people struck down by illnesses that are usually not diagnosed until they are fairly well advanced, report that machines featured in their dreams some time before any physical symptoms appeared. Dream machines are also seen as representing logical thinking. If they are seen as being in perfect working order, then the dreamer is likely to be the sort of person others turn to for advice to see them through a difficult situation. Well-oiled, smooth-running machinery is seen as a sign that the dreamer is more than happy with domestic matters, but to dream of being caught

• •

or injured in a machine is a warning that unhappiness and loss loom large on the horizon.

Maggots are generally thought to be an indication that the dreamer is concerned about death – not a physically imminent one, but the spiritual aspect of passing from one stage of being to another. They can also suggest that the dreamer feels that there is something within him – a thought, an idea, a feeling perhaps – that should not be there, and that is making him feel impure in some way. Their appearance has also been seen as a warning that a lazy acquaintance has been subtly leeching on the dreamer who is only now becoming aware that he is being used.

Memorials can serve as recognition that the dreamer feels a deep-rooted but unspoken, perhaps unacknowledged, nostalgia for a time in life which was much happier than at present. They are also, perhaps, the subconscious's way of taking the reader back to an unpleasant memory that is indelibly imprinted on the dreamer's mind. If this is the case, the dreamer is being told to come to terms with it and to leave it behind if it is not to surface as a ball and chain that will prevent full potential being realized. Romanies believed that to dream of a memorial signified that the dreamer would soon be called upon to be particularly kind to

• •

relations who were threatened with sickness or financial difficulty.

Money is linked to the value the dreamer puts on himself or herself. To see it suggests that he is starting to question that value because there may be a deep-rooted suspicion that he may be selling himself short. To dream of finding money is seen by many as a sign that the dreamer will experience many small worries but that on balance a happy life will be enjoyed. To see oneself paying out cash is a sign of misfortune on the way and if you see yourself counting money and finding yourself short, then if the bills are not already piling up on your desk, it's just a matter of time. It's even worse to see yourself stealing money, for then your finances are in real danger of collapsing.

The **Moon** has, since time immemorial, been seen as representative of the feminine and emotional side of the psyche – which is why it is often referred to as Lady Moon. When she lights up your dreams, she is telling men and women alike that the time is ripe to pay attention to what the feminine side is saying and to pay more attention to emotional thinking than cool logic. It may be that male dreamers who see the Moon are, deep down, afraid of women: the dream tells them not to be. To the female dreamer, the Moon suggests that

• •

she should draw strength from the sorority of other women. According to Gypsies, to see the Moon in an exceptionally starry sky is a sign of great material success, but to see it in anything other than full glory is a sign that disappointment is on the cards, especially where the behaviour of a spouse is concerned.

Murder, generally, suggests that the dreamer is struggling to control some part of his nature or an instinct that he does not trust. If he is the victim then it signifies that his life is way out of kilter and that he must take whatever steps are necessary to restore essential balance. To dream of murdering a parent does not say that the dreamer had an unhappy childhood. Rather, it suggests that the apron strings have not been totally severed as the dreamer would like them to be. Such a dream can persist after the death of both parents, indicating that the dreamer is still too tied emotionally to them. To see a murder warns that inevitable change is in the air and that if the dreamer can grin and bear it, the outcome will not be as bad as was feared.

Nails (the sort we hammer in to hold pieces of wood together, as opposed to the horny attachments to our fingers) are indicative of the dreamer's ability to hold things together. If they are obviously secure, then the

• •

dreamer is confident of this ability, but if they are loose, they may be indicative of a fear that life is about to fall apart. To some analysts, nails are associated with masculinity and sexuality. Again, if they are firm, the dreamer is secure in his sexuality, but if they are falling out, then there may be deep-rooted fears concerning this. Seers of days gone by, believed that to see nails was to be told that you will work hard throughout your life for very little reward, but if the nails are bright and shiny that won't matter to you. Dull or bent nails were thought to herald a bout of illness or a phase when disorder of some sort would rule the day. And to hurt yourself while hammering in a nail was a warning to hold your tongue however tempting it may be to lash out.

Nests suggest that the dreamer treasures safety above all else and in so doing suspects that he or she has become over-reliant emotionally on family and close friends. Traditionally, to dream of an empty nest was thought to be a warning that business may be about to go through a difficult spell, while if there were eggs in it, then investments recently made will give good returns. And nestlings chirruping merrily were thought to denote safe and successful journeys.

Newspapers are believed to be an indication that the dreamer is the sort of person who likes to have all –

and we mean all – the facts before coming to a decision, no matter how trivial. Some interpreters even go so far as saying that different types of newspapers have different meanings. For example, dreaming of a daily broadsheet, suggests that the dreamer believes that the devil is in the detail in all aspects of life, while to dream of the weightier Sundays suggests that the dreamer is the kind of person who can assimilate information without appearing to do so. In the days when newspapers did not enjoy the wide circulation that they do today, it was thought that to dream of them was to be warned that any dishonesty perpetrated in the past would soon be uncovered and the dreamer's reputation badly affected.

Night is the time when most of us relax, sleep and gather the strength needed to see us through the following day. To see it in our dreams is to suggest that the dreamer is becoming aware that the time is drawing close when the decision to make a new beginning will have to be made – shaking off the old and embracing the new. Older generations of analysts believed that to have dreamt of the night was to be warned that oppression was about to blow in, to the detriment of the dreamer's business.

Nooses, with their obvious association with the hangman and the inevitable death that follows, are

● ●

thought to suggest that the dreamer feels trapped, perhaps by his past but more likely by the actions and attitudes of other people. If this interpretation is accepted, then it is up to the dreamer to look to the past, come to terms with it and move on, or to shrug his shoulders at society and get on with life as he thinks it should be lived.

Obelisks indicate that we are aware that we were born with a fundamental nature and that it is up to us to shape it to our best advantage. The more basic the obelisk is, then the more we are aware that there is still a great deal to do. But if it is ornately carved, then the better are we using our creative talents and the more instinctively do we lead our lives. An obelisk seen as being tall and totally unadorned indicates that we are presenting a very cold face to society and the dream warns us to change our ways unless we want to face a cold, lonely future. Obelisks are also phallic symbols and if the dreamer suspects that it has some sort of sexual connotation then its meaning can only be interpreted in the context of the entire dream.

Obituaries may not make as sad a reading in the pages of a book about dreams as they can do in the pages of a newspaper, but they are unwelcome nonetheless. To dream of such a piece of journalism

● ●

presages that duties of an unpleasant nature will fall on the dreamer, while to dream of reading one says that news of an unsettling nature will awaken the dreamer from his daytime reveries.

Obstacles can be either physical barriers that prevent us getting from place to place or emotions that stop us moving on from one situation to another and coping with each one as it appears. To dream of such an obstacle is to be aware that it exists and it is up to the dreamer to find the best way round it. Often, once the subconscious awareness has become a conscious realization, the battle to get over it is more than half-won.

Ornaments can indicate that we feel undervalued in a relationship but that we have it in our power to do something about it. And we should do so very quickly if, like so many ornaments, that relationship is not to be put on a shelf and left there to gather dust. Ornaments can also suggest that the dreamer is of a financially extravagant nature and the dream is a warning to pull in his horns.

Orphans are an expression of the dreamer's feeling of being unwanted, unloved and the resulting vulnerability. To dream of being orphaned is to be

● ●

told that it is time to shake off the invisible apron
strings, stand on our own two feet and accept that
we can't live in the protection of others all our lives. A
dream of being in the company of orphans used to
be thought of as a sign that the dreamer's personal
enjoyment was about to be sacrificed because of
the unhappiness of others.

Parachutes are protective in dreams, suggesting
that whatever life throws at us in our waking lives, we
have sufficient emotional reserves to take it and get
through to the other side safely. They can also indicate
that the dreamer is seeking freedom from an
emotional tie and the subconscious, by making the
parachute appear in a dream, is telling the dreamer
that this is the right course to follow.

Paradise is closely linked to the fact that we all have
it in us to be perfect – or at least we had until life
tainted us with experience. To dream *in Arcadia ego* is
an expression that we are striving to achieve a balance
between the perfection we desire and the knowledge
that none of us can be perfect. On another level, to
dream of paradise is an indication that the dreamer
runs his life well and values honesty above all else. It
also suggests that he or she has the ability to be
successful and happy in whatever field chosen, as

long as the principles by which life is lived at present are stuck to.

Pens serve as an indication that we need to communicate more with other people. If the pen is faulty and cannot be made to work, then it's likely that we have been given some information but have either failed to understand it or feel that we have not been given enough to take the appropriate course of action. The latter is reinforced if we dream that we lay the pen down to find another one but are unable to do so. Romany folk believed that to dream of a pen was to be warned that a love of adventure would lead the dreamer into some serious complications. And a pen that refused to write served as a warning that the dreamer was in danger of being charged with a serious breach of society's moral code.

Photographs, with their associations with times gone by, indicate that the dreamer is looking to the past to help find a solution to a present problem. If dreamers dream they are looking at themselves in a group photograph, they may well be in the process of rethinking relationships or attitudes. When photographs were a novelty, they were sometimes regarded with suspicion. This accounts for earlier interpretations, which include deception creeping up on the dreamer,

● ●

false loyalties, suspicions regarding a partner's fidelity and being the unwitting cause of trouble.

Prostitutes, harlots, whores, (ladies of the night for more prudish readers), hookers – call them what you will – they sell the same thing. Sex. And there's usually (not always) a sexual connotation when they walk the streets in your dreams. To the male, their presence can indicate a compelling, desperate need for a relationship to be brought to sexual fruition. To the woman, dreaming of harlots indicates an unfulfilled need for sexual freedom. To dreamers of both sexes, they can suggest that guilt and sex walk hand in hand in the dreamer's mind. To dream of paying for sexual services is seen as a suggestion that the dreamer is worried lest his or her performance in matters sexual is not up to scratch. While to dream of receiving money in return for sexual favours indicates either that the dreamer believes that sexual relationships come at a cost, or that there is a suspicion about entering into a loving relationship. Maybe both! Other analysts believe that dreams involving such demimondaines tell that the dreamer has a poor self-image and is afraid of giving himself or herself 100 percent not just to sex, but in the workplace, in friendships, in matters of faith, whatever. Interpreters in times gone by believed that when whores and harlots featured in dreams, the dreamer had chosen to seek fulfilment in illicit pleasures and that this would bring about his or her downfall both socially and professionally. And lastly, for an unmarried woman to see a hooker in her dreams said that she would lie about her sexual past in order to impress a new lover and then be found out, the knowledge would fatally poison his love for her.

Quarries suggest that the dreamer is digging deep into his or her personality, hoping to find something lurking there that will help solve a current problem. To dream of tumbling into one, presages some sort of difficulty about to be faced either by the dreamer or someone close to him or her.

Quicksand denotes insecurity and lack of control over events that are seen as moving ahead at a gallop. The dream serves to warn the dreamer that he or she must move quickly if the dream is not to be translated into reality. To see oneself trapped by and sinking into quicksand suggests that the dreamer feels ensnared by a difficult situation of someone else's making.

Radios are a clear sign that communication is dominating the subconscious mind and suggest that the dreamer wants to seek the advice of someone they respect to talk through a problem in the hope of

• •

finding a solution to it. They also suggest a feeling that advice that has been offered so far is not enough. When radios were a pleasant and, to many, an unaffordable diversion, they were said to signify that pleasure and prosperity lay ahead when they appeared in dreams, and that a new friendship would be made that would enhance the dreamer's prospects.

Reflections reflect our self-image, which may be stating the obvious, but that's what they do. They can warn that the dreamer is too concerned with how he or she is perceived by society. If he would only look beyond the superficial and try to explore what is behind what he sees, then he would come to enjoy a greater understanding not just of himself but of society in general.

Resignation indicates that we have given up on something and we are not sure if in doing so we have made a huge gaffe or done the right thing. To see oneself as being resigned to something or resigning from a job says that the dreamer has tried everything to get through a particular situation and is no longer willing to invest the time and energy necessary to do any more. But other factors in the dream may indicate that there is still something that can be done if the dreamer is willing to explore just one last alleyway. Only he or she can decide whether or not to try it.

Rocking is a comfort activity and as such suggests that the dreamer is trying to get in touch with real matters – to cast off the unnecessary trappings of life and rebuild the basics. In doing so, the foundations can be built on to create a more rewarding and consequently much happier life.

Rope on one level suggests that the dreamer is ready to accept the responsibility that life is about to ask him or her to carry. It could be the case, often is, that these responsibilities have already been half-accepted, but that something has held the dreamer back from 100 percent commitment. The dream tells them that now is the hour. If the dreamer is tied to the rope, then perhaps there is a feeling of being constrained, especially at work. But if the dreamer takes the opportunity to stand back and decide what is really important, there is nothing to stop them cutting through the rope and moving on.

Seduction, according to traditional dream analysts, has two or three meanings, depending on the sex of the dreamer. If the dreamer was a young woman and she dreamed that she was being seduced, that was a warning to her to beware of being overinfluenced by attractive extroverts. For the male dreamer, on the other hand, to dream that he was seducing an attractive young woman was a warning that he may be about to stand falsely accused of some misdeed. If the woman being seduced gives in, then she may well be attracted to what he offers on the worldly-goods front rather than the loving one. But if she fights for her honour, then she is, indeed, above reproach and will make him a fine wife.

Sex, according to Freud, is the very stuff of which dreams are made. Many dream symbols could somehow or other be put down to matters sexual no matter how distant or tortuous the connection seems to be. Fair enough, for when a child is born it is almost immediately aware at an obviously unexpressed level that it is no longer part of its mother's body: it has a life of its own and almost immediately the search for warmth, comfort and love begins. At first the mother fulfils these needs, but it is not long before the baby becomes aware that its sexual organs can provide them. At first this is via unintentional contact with them. Later it finds expression in the typical toddler's fascination with his or her own body and later through contact with others. Given this, and society's still sometimes prudish attitude towards sex, it is little wonder that deep-rooted guilt associations are formed and that as the child progresses to adulthood, this guilt is expressed in countless hundreds of thousands of dreams! Briefly, very briefly, dreams of sex allow the mature human to explore aspects of sex that were suppressed at childhood and to enjoy them. It is only when we awaken that guilt re-establishes itself! So sex in dreams is the subconscious's way of balancing this guilt with the natural need for sexual self-expression. Pre-nineteenth-century dream interpreters took a simpler view. To them, to dream of having good, pleasurable sex was a sign that personal relationships, not just sexual ones, were a source of great joy to the dreamer and that there was no reason to worry that they may ever be anything else. To dream of watching others having sex on the other hand, suggested that the dreamer was unable to find fulfilment in his or her relationships – sexual or social. And to dream of having sex and finding it a burden rather than a pleasure signified that the dreamer was thinking about getting involved in a business undertaking but was concerned that if he did, the consequences may be unfortunate to say the least.

Shrouds serve as a warning to the dreamers that they should take better care of themselves as their health may be about to be called into question. They

•••••••••••••••••••••••••••••••••••••••

can also say that a false friend will cause the dreamer some sort of financial hardship and will enjoy seeing the deep distress this causes. If the dream concerns a shroud being removed from a corpse this is a warning that a squabble, if not patched up quickly, could deepen into a bitter argument that will never be completely healed.

Smoke signifies that doubts and fears will puzzle you. Try to ignore them because there really is nothing to worry about, unless you dream that you are overcome with smoke. In that case, a silver-tongued flatterer is about to victimize you.

Spring when dreamed of as suddenly appearing out of nowhere in a dream forewarns that something is not right in the dreamer's life and that whatever it is will soon crawl out of the woodwork and play an increasingly large and unsettling part in things. If the dreamer sees the buds of spring starting to bloom and the season progresses sweetly into summer, then all's well and the dreamer can look forward to prosperous times in business and the company of good friends.

Taxes suggest that the dreamer is aware that everything in life has to be paid for in some way or

• •

other. If there is no difficulty in raising the money to pay the dream tax and if the dreamer is happy to pay it, then this can be taken as a sign that the dreamer is reasonably content with life – even if the pleasures he most enjoys are of the forbidden variety. To be seen struggling to pay or to begrudge the money is a sign of guilt. A refusal to pay tax indicates that the dreamer takes an unconventional view of life and lives it according to his own rules rather than those respected by the rest of us.

Teasing indicates an awareness that society is frowning on the way the dreamer conducts himself, if he or she is the one being teased. Curiously, if the dreamer is the teaser rather than the teased, this is thought to be the subconscious's way of highlighting the dreamer's own idiosyncrasies. To dream of teasing can also be a sign of insecurity and a slowly dawning awareness of the dreamer's doubts and fears about some aspect of their personalities. Such doubts and fears probably result from a childhood experience that was long forgotten. Remember, the memory forgets nothing. In centuries gone by, teasing was thought to denote a cheerful, well-mannered personality that would make the dreamer much sought after in society and successful in business. But for a young woman to

• •

dream that she was being teased was a sign that she would give her heart too quickly and that she would live to regret it.

Thistles waken the dreamer to the fact that he may be perceived as being defiant and vindictive by colleagues and acquaintances and that unless he puts his house in order, this view could start to have some serious ramifications. Single thistles can indicate that the road ahead is plagued with minor difficulties, while to dream of a field of thistles suggests that the dreamer should follow another path altogether. Gypsies believed that if the dreamer saw himself hacking his way through a dense undergrowth of huge thistles, then he was about to become involved in a lawsuit that he would most likely lose.

Tornadoes say that disappointment is about to blow into your life, especially if you have been banking on some long-laid plans coming to successful fruition. They won't! Tornadoes can also be seen as a suggestion that the dreamer feels threatened by a surge of emotions that could blow him off course. This interpretation can be taken as a suggestion that he is aware that if he makes some changes then he will be able to keep his feet on the ground and weather the storm.

● ●

Toys tell the dreamer that the family will be a source of ever-increasing joy, as long as the toys are in reasonable condition. If they are broken then some sort of heartbreak is foretold. To see children playing with toys says that happiness will smile on the dreamer's marriage. And to see oneself giving away toys suggests that friends and acquaintances will, for some unknown reason, give one the cold shoulder. Toys are also thought to highlight the creative part of the dreamer's life and they may point to the fact that the dreamer is open to new ideas and new ways in which they can relate to other people. And it may be that when toys feature in a dream, then the dreamer is being told that he or she is working too hard and to take some time off to relax and have some fun.

Umbrellas – the word comes from two Spanish words that mean 'shade the lady' – shelter us from the elements, sun as well as rain. When seen in dreams they indicate that we enjoy the shelter offered to us by a friend or a colleague. They can also be seen as a sign to the dreamer that improving skills and further education could be the keys to providing shelter later in life. To dream of carrying a rolled-up umbrella in the rain suggests that business plans are about to go awry, while a leaky one denotes quarrels with loved ones.

● ●

Undressing puts us in touch with our sexual being and indicates a need to reveal our true feelings about someone or perhaps about a situation concerning which we have not been true to ourselves. If we are watching another person getting undressed, it may be a sign that while we are aware that we should be more sensitive to other people's feelings we don't do much about it. So the dream serves as a wake-up call to become less self-centred emotionally than we are. To dream that we are taking another's clothes off indicates a need to understand something about ourselves, which is slowly stirring in the very depths of our being. Dream analysts of times past believed that to dream that you are undressing denoted a rift with a loved one because of the scandalous behaviour of one or other of you. And to see someone else undressing presaged bad luck in love and money, while to dream of being undressed by someone else was thought to be a sign that flirtation would lead to romantic disaster.

Urgency, when it is the feeling that stands out most in a dream, can be taken as a warning that you have overlooked something very small. But unlike the rolling stone, it will gather moss and become bigger and bigger and assume an importance out of all proportion to its original size. So if you have this dream sensation, go through the fine detail of your life, leaving no stone unturned. Other factors in the dream may give a clue as to where you should be looking. If you are being asked for urgent advice, then something may well be about to crop up that will require a little financial juggling on your part.

Vaults can suggest that the dreamer is aware that something of a sexual nature may be stirring and may soon come to play a significant part in his or her life. They can also represent our store of collective knowledge, something that increases as we age and which is always there when we need to draw on it. Indeed, to be seen going down into a vault suggests that we are already aware of this and are on the verge of exploring it to see how it can help us in several aspects of our life. To be seen burying something in a vault was seen by Gypsies as a sign that dreamers would soon suffer a sad loss. And to dream of burying something valuable in a vault was a warning to be on the lookout lest someone try to cheat you out of money or land.

Visits, in the sense that someone is seen calling on the dreamer, indicate that we are aware that what we need – be it comfort, information or love – is out there waiting if only we knew where to look. That is if the

• •

dreamer knows the visitor. If it is a stranger who comes knocking at the door, then he or she may represent a facet of our personality that has long been unrecognized, but that is now trying to establish itself in the dreamer's consciousness. To be seen making a visit is significant of a need to widen the horizons if life is to be lived to the full. According to folklore, to dream of a visitor clad in black is to be warned of accidents waiting to happen. And if the visitor is obviously weary after a long journey, then although the actions of family or friends may cause displeasure, it would be better to keep your feelings to yourself, for if you give them voice they may cause wounds that will never be healed.

Wakes, be they of a suitably solemn nature or the more raucous traditional Irish variety, tell the dreamer that he is subconsciously aware of a need to grieve over something that has gone from his life. It may not be a person: perhaps it is a phase of life, a friendship, whatever – but something gone for ever. And once the grieving is over, the dream says that it is time to move on, to grasp new opportunities, accept that ageing is an unavoidable part of life, make new friends... Wakes also suggest that the dreamer is acknowledging that the support of friends and colleagues is needed if a disappointment is to be overcome. Traditionally, dreams in which a wake plays a central part told the dreamer that a long-looked-forward-to engagement would have to be cancelled to make room in the diary for a meeting of an unpleasant kind. And for an unmarried young woman to dream that she sees her young man at a wake suggests that despite her best intentions to keep herself chaste until she walks down the aisle, his silver-tongued smoothness will persuade her otherwise – something she will come to regret deeply.

Whirlpools suggest that the dreamer is about to be caught up in danger, especially if he is involved in running a business. It could be that the ripples caused by some sort of personal scandal will cause customers and colleagues to think again before finally committing themselves to a project that was almost signed and sealed.

Winter, when it blows into a dream, warns that a bout of ill health is on the cards and that things on the business front may become a bit frosty before a little sunshine sets in. Gypsies believed that in days immediately following a winter dream, no matter how hard the dreamer tries to achieve something, his efforts will yield absolutely nothing.

A-Z OF DREAMS

● ●

X marks the spot in dreams as it is said to do in life. If that X is dreamed of as being on a treasure map, then according to Gypsy tradition the goals you have set yourself are in sight and will earn you your just reward. A more modern interpretation is that to see an X is to be warned that something recently done in all innocence may turn out to be unwise, but that it is not too late to undo it before any damage results. If the sign is more of a cross than a recognizable letter of the alphabet, then it may indicate that a sacrifice of some sort has recently been or is about to be made.

Yawning in dreams can indicate the same as it does in life – boredom! What it is that the dreamer is bored with only he or she can say. It could be a job, a friendship, a love affair, whatever. Yawning can also suggest that the dreamer is forming an opinion about something but is not yet ready to give voice to it and will not do so until every option has been examined and thoroughly thought through. On another level, yawning can also be seen as a warning to control one's own abusive tendencies or to try to bring the abusive behaviour of another under control. To see someone else yawn is to be warned that a close friend may be about to fall seriously ill or get into financial trouble. Whichever it is, the dreamer will be called upon for help, which will be gladly given.

● ●

Yielding in a dream is to be aware that a situation has reached a point where only direct confrontation with another person would seem to be the answer, but to know that such confrontation will be ultimately useless. In this circumstance it may be best to step aside and go along with the majority, even though you know they're wrong! On a spiritual level, yielding can suggest that the dreamer has been aware that there is more to life than material success and that the time is right to do something about it. Gypsies believe that to dream of being yearned for by a friend or lover is a sign of assured happiness. And if you dream of yearning for a particular person then your choice of spouse was or will be perfect.

Zips are often seen in dreams as symbolic of our ability to develop relationships with other people. Put simply, open zips suggest an open nature, the ability to make friends easily and to keep the fires of friendship burning for ever. On the other hand, a closed zip indicates a tendency to hold back from offering the hand of friendship until you are absolutely sure. Beware that in doing so you are not seen as something of a cold fish.